A Journey with Two Mystics

A Journey with Two Mystics

Conversations between a Girardian and a Wattsian

MATTHEW J. DISTEFANO
AND
MICHAEL MACHUGA

Foreword by Ric Machuga
Afterword by Ben Fullerton

RESOURCE *Publications* • Eugene, Oregon

A JOURNEY WITH TWO MYSTICS
Conversations between a Girardian and a Wattsian

Copyright © 2017 Matthew J. Distefano and Michael Machuga. All rights reserved. Except for brief quotations in critical publications or reviews, no part of this book may be reproduced in any manner without prior written permission from the publisher. Write: Permissions, Wipf and Stock Publishers, 199 W. 8th Ave., Suite 3, Eugene, OR 97401.

Resource Publications
An Imprint of Wipf and Stock Publishers
199 W. 8th Ave., Suite 3
Eugene, OR 97401

www.wipfandstock.com

PAPERBACK ISBN: 978-1-5326-1709-6
HARDCOVER ISBN: 978-1-4982-4153-3
EBOOK ISBN: 978-1-4982-4152-6

Manufactured in the U.S.A.   MARCH 24, 2017

Scripture quotations, unless otherwise noted, taken from the *New Revised Standard Version* and are copyright © 1989 by the Division of Christian Education of the National Council of Churches of Christ in the U.S.A. and are used by permission.

To Lyndsay and Speri,
and to all the sojourners of the world

"It is not our part to master all the tides of the world, but to do what is in us for the succour of those years wherein we are set, uprooting the evil in the fields that we know, so that those who live after may have clean earth to till. What weather they shall have is not ours to rule."[1]

~ GANDALF

---

1. Tolkien, *Return of the King*, 861.

Contents

Foreword by Ric Machuga | *xiii*
Matthew's Acknowledgments | *xvii*
Michael's Acknowledgments | *xix*
Matthew's Introduction: Friendship and Letters | *xxi*
Michael's Introduction: Growing Tired of Religion | *xxv*

ACT I: EXPLORING THE HUMAN

Letter 1 We Are Each Other | 3
Letter 2 Human Consciousness | 8
Letter 3 A Clarification of Mimetic Desire | 11
Letter 4 The Pitfalls of Self-Consciousness | 15
Letter 5 Positive Mimesis and a Relational God | 18
     First Refrain | 22

ACT II: EXPLORING SALVATION

Letter 6 Heaven is At-Hand | 33
Letter 7 A Changing Understanding of What It Means to Be Saved | 37
Letter 8 Sin, Salvation, and Belief in Jesus | 41
Letter 9 Jesus is Lord, Period! | 46

Letter 10   Why I am a Universalist | 50
    Second Refrain | 54

ACT III: EXPLORING HELL

Letter 11   The Authority of Scripture and Some Really Bad News | 63
Letter 12   Hell: Eternal Torture or Annoying Distraction? | 69
Letter 13   What in the Hell Is Hell? | 73
Letter 14   Musings about Justice | 78
Letter 15   Justice, Freedom, and the Implications for Humankind | 82
    Third Refrain | 86

ACT IV: EXPLORING REALITY

Letter 16   The "Meaning" of Life | 97
Letter 17   Our Theology is not God, but it can Certainly Point in Her Direction | 100
Letter 18   Meditation and Mindfulness | 104
Letter 19   God and the Universe are One: Forming a Holistic Worldview | 108
Letter 20   The World is "Out There" | 113
Afterword   Moving Beyond Words by Ben Fullerton | 117
Bibliography | 121

Foreword

BY RIC MACHUGA

"*Come to me, all you that are weary and are carrying heavy burdens, and I will give you rest . . . for I am gentle and humble in heart, and you will find rest for your souls. For my yoke is easy, and my burden is light.*"

~ JESUS, IN MATTHEW 11:28–30

These are familiar words to anyone who grew up in an evangelical church, as Matthew Distefano and Michael Machuga did. By the time they were ten or eleven, both were able to identify these words as the words of Jesus. And both received a simple childlike comfort.

Yet, as they describe it, by the time they were in their mid-twenties, that comfort was beginning to wane. Why? With respect to the specific details and events leading to their discomfort, I can only speculate. Perhaps it occurred one night when they were reading their Bibles with their childlike faith and came across these verses: "Then he [Jesus] began to reproach the cities in which most of his deeds of power had been done, because they did not repent. 'Woe to you, Chorazin! Woe to you, Bethsaida! . . . I tell you, on the day of judgment it will be more tolerable for Tyre and Sidon than for you . . . you will be brought down to Hades" (Matt 11:20–23). All of a sudden Jesus' words seem more like threats than comforting words for children. "Will I," they may have thought to themselves, "Be 'brought down to Hades'? How long must I pray to be forgiven for getting angry at my big sister today?" Even if they had yet to understand exactly what it meant to "be brought down to Hades," they certainly understood that it wasn't good news.

But in not too many years—and now I am no longer speculating because the authors tell us—they were told exactly what it meant: Being "brought down to Hades" meant suffering torment in the everlasting fires of hell! All of a sudden, the good news of the Gospel didn't appear so good to these thoughtful and empathetic young men.

When young evangelicals hear that their church believes that those who die "without Christ" will be condemned to an afterlife of everlasting pain and suffering, my hunch is that they self-divide into three groups.

One third "hear the bad news," but don't believe it threatens them because they have "prayed the prayer" confessing Jesus as Lord and Savior. Hell is for others, not them, so why worry?

One third have "prayed the prayer," yet their worry remains. So they work harder—pray more, go to church more, "witness" more, go on short-term mission trips, swear off swearing and R-rated movies. Yet, nothing seems to help—the threat of everlasting, conscious torment in the fires of hell still wakes them in the middle of the night. So, they study the Bible more carefully, seeking relief. But none comes. In fact, it gets worse when they learn the Bible is full of passages about the "wrath of God." *Do all of these refer to hell? If so, then I'm in a heap of trouble.* And it only gets worse when they discover that Jesus had a "counter-cultural" understanding of God's wrath. It's not the pimps and prostitutes who are going to hell; it's the establishment good guys—scribes and Pharisees and

Foreword

teachers of the law—who are the primary target of God's wrath! "That sounds like me," they say to themselves. "Have I only made matters worse by working so hard to be good?"

The final third say to themselves, "To hell with hell. If, as I am told by my church, the Bible clearly teaches that the hope of everlasting joy with Jesus in heaven *requires* that many must suffer the everlasting fires of hell, then maybe the Bible isn't such a 'Good Book' after all. I should start looking at other forms of spirituality."

Now, I do not doubt that many young people move back and forth between these groups of thirds, especially between the second and the third. But if you find yourself firmly in the first group, then it is highly unlikely that this book will speak to you. On the other hand, if you are one of those "moving targets"—some days you find yourself in group two, other days in group three—then you will find Matthew and Michael to be kindred spirits.

Though I should be clear that to be a "kindred spirit" does *not* mean that you must deny the existence of hell. Neither of our authors deny that it is a "terrible thing to suffer the wrath of God." All they deny is that God's "wrath" is a *wholly* vengeful and punitive wrath that never ends because it never achieves its goal of bringing *all* to Christ. No, God's wrath is a gracious wrath. "One day *every* knee shall bow and *every* tongue confess that Jesus Christ is Lord" (Rom 14:11—emphasis mine). This is the hope to which this book points.

And if you come to share this hope, who knows, since Matthew maintains an active web and social media presence, you may even become his online friend. On the other hand, making contact with my son Michael may be a little harder since he is a self-confessed "lazy-ass" whose online presence is minimal. But, rest assured, he's a pretty nice guy who will secretly welcome a kick in the butt! So seek, and ye shall find.

Matthew's Acknowledgments

First, I want to acknowledge my dear friend and coauthor of this book, Michael Machuga. For years, he has been the best best-friend anyone in the world could have. Michael has helped shape me in so many ways, not only philosophically and theologically, but personally as well. Without him, not only would this book not exist, but I fear neither of my first two publications would have even been written. At least, both would have been lacking in many ways.

I also have to thank the two beautiful girls that I share my life with. My wife Lyndsay has been my life partner and my inspiration, while my daughter Elyse has, in so many wonderful ways, followed closely in her footsteps. Behind Matthew the author are two girls who keep me sane, who keep me going, and who always know how to make my day brighter and full of joy.

I owe a debt of gratitude to all of my theological mentors out there; folks like Michael Hardin, Bradley Jersak, James Alison, Thomas Talbott, and many others. And even though I never had the chance to meet him, I must also acknowledge the late René Girard. It is he who is ultimately to thank for many of the thoughts I put forth throughout this book.

A huge thank you is owed to Ric Machuga (foreword) and Ben Fullerton (afterword), who each contributed their gift of

Matthew's Acknowledgments

wordsmithery to this project. And to Lindsey Paris-Lopez and Dan Wilkinson, who did a masterful job editing our letters: thank you!

Lastly, I would like to make mention of the many wonderful people who engage with me on my blog and Facebook page. Since I've decided to "do theology" in the public square, I have met so many amazing people. Folks who initially come to mind are "Barefoot" Stephen Morris, Tom VanGaalen, Josh Felts, Jeff Turner, the Miller family (Caleb, Gabby, Mike, and Marilyn), Jim Rogers, Mark Rosen, Greg and Heather Clark, Dan Hinkle, Greg Vadala, the Hardin family (Michael, Lorri, Arwen, and Melian), David Reynard, Simon Wilson, "Trilobite" Russ Jacobson, Sam Mathew, Chris Thomas, Ken Kammerer, Ben Fullerton, Giovanni Scavetta, Rob Grayson, Eric Alexander, Heather Clark, Michelle Collins, Megan Jones, Claire Reiter, Brian Cordova, David Markham, Jamal Jivanjee, Ralph Polendo, Brandon Chase, David Mosher, Aaron Hugh Glenn, Patricia Mikkelson, David Hazard, Josiah Strode, Mark Ballard, Robert Lofgren, Lisa Stratton-Stevens, Doug Stuart, Fred-Allen Self (an additional shout out for maintaining my website, allsetfree.com), Ravi Holy, Wendy and Don Francisco, Joel "Drunk in Love" Weaver, Terri-Anne Williams, Jerry Nkwe, Kevin Reese, The O'Neil family, Aidan Parle, Mark Stone, Chuck McKnight (the "Hippie Heretic"), Carlos Sawyer, Nathan Smith, Mike Rough, Dominic and Amanda Moes, Peter Bell, Brandan Robertson, and many more. If I missed you, it is not because I have failed to notice you; it is simply because there are so many people who have had a positive impact on my life that I do not have the space. To everyone who supports me, though, thank you! May the peace of Christ Jesus comfort you always.

Michael's Acknowledgments

I don't know how to rank the importance of the people who have helped with this book so in alphabetical order by first name:

My mother, Kathy Machuga, is perhaps not directly responsible for the words on these pages, but instead is responsible for my understanding of what love ought to be. And if God is not as loving as she is, it will be a great disappointment.

Matthew Distefano, coauthor and comrade in life, put the most work into this project. In addition to writing at least half of the material, he did the vast majority of the proofreading and editing, as well as the leg work needed to get us published.

Ric Machuga, father and author of the foreword, is responsible for my interest in philosophy and religion. Growing up, most every bike ride, or hike, or ski trip, or morning spent flying RC airplanes was accompanied by a discussion about life's big ideas. He is also my model for what it means to be a good man.

Speri Machuga is my wife and the person I most enjoy being around. I crave her encouragement the most. Without her support, I would lack the courage to write this book.

Matthew's Introduction
Friendship and Letters

"Friendship arises out of mere Companionship when two or more of the companions discover that they have in common some insight or interest or even taste which the others do not share and which, till that moment, each believed to be his own unique treasure (or burden). The typical expression of opening Friendship would be something like, 'What? You too? I thought I was the only one.'"[1]

~ C.S. Lewis

"To want friendship is a great fault. Friendship ought to be a gratuitous joy, like the joys afforded by art, or life."[2]

~ Simone Weil

---

1. Lewis, *Four Loves*, 65.
2. Weil, *First and Last Notebooks*, 43.

Matthew's Introduction

"I am glad you are here with me. Here at the end of all things, Sam."[3]

~ Frodo Baggins

It is one thing to have a best friend but it is quite another to have a person like Michael as one. From fairly early on in my theological journey, he has been there for and with me—both as a mentor and a student. But most of all, he has been a most blessed confidant and someone I will always cherish.

It is a funny thing how Michael and I became close, as it was not really a "love at first sight" kind of friendship. While we grew up in the same church, had some of the same friends, and chatted from time to time, we never really got to know each other all too well. It was not until after I had deconstructed some of my prior Christian beliefs that I found out that Michael had been doing a very similar thing. This triggered what has been, for us, a friendship that has since only grown and blossomed.

Since the time our companionship first took off, I have spent nearly every Thursday evening on Michael's back porch, with the bonfire crackling, the red wine flowing, and chatting about whatever the topic du jour happened to be that week. Our discussions have generally lasted for two hours, and have covered everything from theology and philosophy, to culture and politics. My Thursday nights have been one of the things that I look forward to most in life. And yet, after a time, we both realized that there was something missing from our bonfire explorations. We needed a little change of pace.

Sometime in 2015, Michael and I decided to do something to structure our ramblings a bit more. The most obvious thing for us was to take the spirit of Thursday night and put it into *written* form—the best we could anyway. After all, we are both highly introverted, so speaking and engaging directly with others, face to face, was out of the question. But, in written word, now that was a

---

3. Tolkien, *Return of the King*, 926.

Matthew's Introduction

different matter. And so, we decided to immortalize our thoughts in *this* way, which, if you ask me, is a nice little mark to make on human history.

Now, let me say a word about the format of this collection . . .

For the most part, this is a compilation of letters that are placed into appropriate "collections." We are calling these "acts" (as in a play) and they will, broadly speaking, each cover one topic. The first is on "what it means to be human," the second on "salvation," and so on. We will insert a few "refrains" from time to time in order to explore various digressions. That is just who we are, both enjoying a good rabbit hole from time to time. And that is also what makes this is an exploration of sorts, where nothing is too strict. At times, we may wander. So, as Michael will talk about in his introduction, think of this, not as a scholarly work per se, but rather, as a candid look into the hearts and minds of a couple of sojourners, two nomads wandering in the desert.

What we hope to discover in our journey together is that if we pay attention in life, we can find commonalities between what, on the surface at least, seem like disparate ideas. Yet, while Michael and I agree on many things, including the ultimate reconciliation of humanity to God, we do not necessarily agree on all the details of how that happens. But, that is okay, because do any two people, really?

That said, the ultimate safety of the universe allows us to have the freedom to explore things that we would not likely explore should we think otherwise. At least, that was always my experience growing up in a church that taught if you happen to not draw the correct conclusions, you were going to sizzle and pop atop the unholy barbecue down below. It is difficult to explore anything in the infinite cosmos when that sort of threat is always lurking in the shadows of your mind.

But now I'm free from all that nonsense, and where there is freedom there is growth.

These letters, then, should help those who find resonance with our words grow, in one way or another.

Matthew's Introduction

So, my advice for you, the reader, is that you take your time and enjoy our discussions. They should provide you with a lot to chew on, that is, if you are a seeker like the two of us. And since you are actually reading my introduction, my guess is that you are. My hope for you, then, is that it helps you in your own journey. After all, we are all on one so we might as well share in the experiences.

"Peace, peace to you,
And peace to the one who helps you!
For your God is the one who helps you."
~ 1 Chronicles 12:18

Matthew J. Distefano
Chico, Ca
7/13/2016

Michael's Introduction
Growing Tired of Religion

"I am in fact a Hobbit (in all but size). I like gardens, trees, and unmechanized farmlands; I smoke a pipe, and like good plain food."[1]

~ J.R.R. TOLKIEN

"Now I'm no biologist, but it seems to make a lot of sense that slow lives, as well as being enjoyable, are long lives. One only has to think of the example of the tortoise for proof of this theory from the animal world."[2]

~ TOM HODGKINSON

It is only on Matthew's energy that I would ever write a book, for I am sort of a lazy person. I do what needs to be done in life—work the "nine to five," for example—but have very little drive to "better

---

1. From a letter to Deborah Webster (October 25, 1958).
2. Hodgkinson, "Live Lazy, Live Long," para. 1.

myself." I am not sure what to think of this, to be honest. I would never promote laziness, but in *one sense* every person is already perfect, and needs no addition or refining. No amount of learning or accomplishing adds anything to a person's value, but learning and accomplishing certainly provides complexity to this dance of life, and that is self-evidently good.

Pardon my language, but my writing style reflects this half-assed approach to life. I read selfishly, really only in order to understand big ideas for myself, and not necessarily to pass on the knowledge to others. Because of this, I tend to write from the hip. And while I am pretty certain I have got things in order, in case I don't, then I have Matthew, Lindsey Paris-Lopez, and Dan Wilkinson as competent editors.

So fear not!

This borderline apathy is reflected in my approach to religion as well. I simply do not have the energy to be a Christian Arminian anymore (Arminianism asserting that human beings have a certain sort of free will and that through this will can reject God's grace forever). I grew up in the Evangelical Church and tried to be a good little boy for roughly twenty-five years. And while I was able to keep this up for a while, dogma and moralism eventually wore me down, and I felt forced to find a more satisfying, liberating view of God elsewhere—in the "religions" of the East, for example. If you *must* label me, I am fine with either Buddhist or Christian Universalist, but in truth, I am probably a little bit of both.

Now, thinking back to my Arminian days, I must say that my biggest beef with it (although some will no doubt object) is that it demands a doing of something, a work of some sort. It requires a decision to be *made*.

Now, or else . . .

That "or else," as I was so emphatically told, was eternal conscious torment (from henceforth referred to as ECT), burning alive for all eternity, miraculously kept alive by some force or mechanism science could never have an answer for.

Because "justice," or something.

Michael's Introduction

It becomes dubious to say, then, that God, as understood through this lens, is truly a God of grace. And while perhaps many from this tradition would freely admit that they do not primarily characterize God as such, opting instead to place the greatest emphasis on honor or justice, they certainly talk about grace an awful lot.

Grace for them, the ones who "get it right," that is.

For a guy like me, this was simply too exhausting to even try to decipher.

Is this pathetic? Is it pathetic that such a decision seemed to require so much energy? I'll allow you to decide. But, I guess it is because I did not—and do not—see how this grand decision is not ultimately absurd. It barely seems like a decision at all, for if people were *truly* informed about the nature of God, as I feel I am now, and what it would mean to reject God, who except for the *insane* would choose against God? Where would a decision like this come from if not a place of mental or spiritual enslavement? Certainly God is more gracious than to allow our eternity to hinge on this type of "choice," or, as Eric Reitan puts it:

> If I exercise my libertarian freedom . . . dooming myself to the outer darkness without reason, I sincerely hope that God would act to stop me—just as I hope a friend would stop me if I decided to leap from a rooftop for no reason. I would not regard the actions of that friend as a violation of any valuable freedom, but would see it as a welcome antidote to arbitrary stupidity.[3]

I could go on and on about this, but enough ranting.

As Matthew stated, this book is conversational and speculative, and certainly not to be taken as scholarly. It does model, however, what I feel should be the spirit of every conversation or "argument"—agreement with a little pushback, and even some poking fun at one another from time to time. Every person has something good to say, and it is better to assume someone to be on the right track in at least one regard. But do not assume they

---

3. Reitan, "Human Freedom," 137.

Michael's Introduction

are perfect. Critics could point out that it is easy for two Universalists to have a civil conversation. After all, what is there to disagree about? Well, just because we agree on the end of the story does not mean we necessarily agree on the plot that gets us there. I have yet to meet *any* two people who have an identical experience of God and the nature of reality. Hence, everyone has a unique relationship with God, even if they do not know it or acknowledge it, and that really should excite everyone. I believe that someday it will.

"The Lord bless you and keep you;
The Lord make his face to shine upon you,
And be gracious to you;
The Lord lift up his countenance upon you,
And give you peace."

~ Numbers 6:24–26

Michael Machuga
Paradise, Ca
9/19/16

ACT I

Exploring the Human

Letter 1

We Are Each Other

Michael,

I am entitling this letter "We Are Each Other," because I believe that it is a fitting answer to a fundamental question: *What does it mean to be human?* I will begin by thinking in strictly anthropological terms, answering through what I will call a Girardian lens (i.e., as a mimetic theorist). Later, we can explore the interconnected relationship between humanity and divinity, but, as I said in *All Set Free*, "If we ask 'Who is God?' before "Who is man?' how can we not end up creating a god of our own design? We must discover who we are before we make any attempt to put our finger on God."[1] So, that is where we will begin, with the human.

Over the course of history, many great minds have attempted to answer this crucial question. For Kant, humanity resided in our ability to have rationality. Go all the way back to Aristotle and you will hear that having an end goal and possessing speech is what defines "man." For the mimetic theorist, the Greek word *mimesis*, or "to imitate," is at the heart of it. That is to say, we are creatures of imitation—and primarily non-consciously. To put it in overly simplified terms, we are all copies of one another. Alan Watts notices:

---

1. Distefano, *All Set Free*, 7.

Act I: Exploring the Human

> We seldom realize, for example, that our most private thoughts and emotions are not actually our own. For we think in terms of languages and images which we did not invent, but which were given to us by our society. We copy emotional reactions from our parents . . . Our societal environment has this power just because we do not exist apart from a society. Society is our extended mind and body.[2]

And not only do we imitate the behavior of our fellow members of society, but also their desires. Thus, René Girard—the father of mimetic theory—coined the term "interdividual."[3] So, when thinking about what a "person" is, think in terms of interdividual rather than individual.

When we think of our "self," we must first discuss the relationships we hold. We must focus on those we look up to, admire, and praise. Girard teaches:

> We are constituted by the other, that is, by parents, authority figures, peers, rivals whom we internalize as models and who become the unconscious basis of our desires. This does not mean that freedom of the will is not possible. Humankind as created in the image of God is not intended to be *identical* to the other or exist in *slavish subservience* to the other. However, since we learn first and primarily through mimesis, our freedom depends on being constituted by the other.[4]

What Girard is arguing is that any freedom this "self" has is *because* we share desires with the other, otherwise our desires would be on fixed objects, or in other words, a form of instinct.[5] *So who, specifically, are the "others" that I am talking about?* They are the people closest to us.[6] Without being a husband, father, son, brother, friend, colleague, mentor, counselor, student, and aspiring to be

---

2. Watts, *The Book*, 70.
3. See book III of Girard's *Things Hidden Since the Foundation of the World*.
4. Girard, *I See Satan*, 137.
5. Ibid., 15.
6. Ibid., 137.

a follower of the risen Christ, who am I? What am I? My identity would be lost, a shadow of its former self. As I have meditated on this, it has become more and more confirming. I am my relationships. We *all* are.

This may sound like some new-age mumbo jumbo to some—American Christians, for example, who have been conditioned by our post-Kantian world to believe we are all autonomous individuals—but it is not. Far from it, in fact, as this worldview actually has strong biblical support. Pardon the proof-texting, but here are some verses from both the Hebrew and Christian Bible. (All emphasis mine.)

- Gen 1:26–27: "Then God said, 'Let us make *humankind in our image*, according to our likeness; and let them have dominion over the fish of the sea, and over the birds of the air, and over the cattle, and over all the wild animals of the earth, and over every creeping thing that creeps upon the earth.' So God created *humankind in his image*, in the image of God he created them; male and female he created them."

- Mark 12:29: "Hear, O Israel: the Lord our God, the Lord is *one*."

- Matthew 25:40: "Truly I tell you, just as you did it to one of the *least of these* who are members of my family, you did it to *me*."

- John 1:1–5: "In the beginning was the *Logos*, and the *Logos* was with God, and the *Logos* was God. He was in the beginning with God. *All things* came into being through him, and without him *not one thing* came into being. What has come into being in him was life, and the life was the light of *all people*."

- Rom 9:2–3: "I have great sorrow and unceasing anguish in my heart. For I could wish that I myself were *accursed and cut off from Christ for the sake of my own people*, my kindred according to the flesh."

ACT I: Exploring the Human

- 1 Cor 12:13: "For in the *one* Spirit we were all baptized into *one* body—Jews or Greeks, slaves or free—and were *all made to drink* of one Spirit."
- Eph 4:6: "One God and Father of *all*, who is above *all* and through *all* and in *all*."
- Col 1:16–18: "For in him *all things* in heaven and on earth were created, things visible and invisible, whether thrones or dominions or rulers or powers—*all things* have been created through him and for him. He himself is before *all things*, and in him *all things* hold together. He is the head of the body, the church; he is the beginning, the firstborn from the dead, so that he might come to have first place in *everything*."

Not only do we find passages that speak to humanity's interdividualism in Scripture, but we also witness how the behavior of the apostles matches such a worldview. In Acts 4:32–37, we learn how believers were "of one heart and soul," even offering all of their possessions for others to share. It reads as a voluntary communism of sorts, where what's mine is literally yours—*without coercion from the State of course*. As theologian David Bentley Hart notices, "When Christianity arrived in Edessa, for instance, its adherents promptly became a kind of mendicant order, apparently owning nothing much at all. In the words of that very early manual of Christian life, the *Didache*, a Christian must never claim that anything is his own property, but must own all things *communally* with his brethren (4:9–12)."[7] This is, admittedly, an over-simplification, but my point is that for the early Christian autonomy was not something that played into their worldview, but rather, that they were of "one body" (see Rom 12:5 and 1 Cor 12:12).

So, it is not as if this idea of interdividualism is new. Rather, it is the emphasis on autonomy and rabid individualism that is the more modern idea. It basically began with William Ockham in the twelfth and thirteenth centuries but then became really solidified

---

7. Hart, "Christ's Rabble," para. 11.

by Immanuel Kant, four centuries later.[8] Hardly "Christian orthodoxy," I know—more like a product of the Enlightenment.

Let me conclude with an autobiographical mention, as I think it drives home the point that we are indeed products of each other. When we went through our deconstruction and subsequent reconstruction phase in life's journey,[9] I must admit that had we gone it alone, I do not know how we would have gotten through it all, as I imagine our sanity would have been challenged even more than it was. That is to say, we leaned on each other greatly during those tenuous times. Furthermore, there would have also been thoughts and ideas that would never have blossomed had we not enjoyed our countless bonfires at your home. So, because of that reality, how much of what I now believe about God, for example, is directly due to *your* contributions? If you think even more broadly, how much of what *you* believe is influenced by your dad?[10] I think you see where I could go with this . . .

I am, of course, interested in what you have to say regarding the human species. Where do you begin when thinking about what defines humanity? I look forward to hearing your response.

"For I am convinced that nothing will be able to separate us from the love of God in Christ Jesus our Lord."
~ ROMANS 8:38–39

Grace and Peace, my friend,

Matthew

---

8. Machuga, *Three Theological Mistakes*, 179–80.

9. What I am referring to here is how both Michael and I began with one set of Christian beliefs, but through diligent questioning, came to abandon them, replacing them with beliefs that actually stood the test of such inquiry.

10. Michael's father, Ric Machuga taught philosophy for over thirty years at Butte College. He is also the author of *Three Theological Mistakes: How to Correct Enlightenment Assumptions about God, Miracles, and Free Will.*

Letter 2

Human Consciousness

Matthew,

I will be addressing the matter of "what it means to be human" in just a moment, but first, I wanted to back up a bit and mention why I tend to *gravitate* toward Buddhist teachings. In short, it is because of my hesitance in determining whether Christianity or Buddhism has the most exciting news to tell. If I *had* to choose which faith tradition's language best describes salvation, for instance, it would be Buddhism's. I suppose because, of the two, Buddhism offers the clearest path to direct intercourse with God. What Buddhism makes obvious is that any profound spiritual encounter can be characterized by a union of the experience and the experiencer, of the knower and the known. This is what Buddhism calls nirvana.

Yet, perhaps I am comparing Buddhism to a strawman of what true Christianity is supposed to look like, because in all honesty, what Christians such as yourself call the kingdom of heaven, is a very similar notion. That is to say, both nirvana and the kingdom of God/heaven are all "at-hand," and both require an inward and outward peace of mind, body, and soul. Of these, though, I find the language of the Buddhist to be more compelling. But let us not place any labels on me quite yet; they tend to get in the way of things.

Allow me to offer a few quick autobiographical snapshots of what I mean by this predominantly Eastern notion of a "union of the experience and experiencer," and then we'll move on to the question at-hand. You see, the third most heavenly times of my life are when I am on my dirt-bike, enveloped in the environment and pure, unadulterated speed. Every turn is a pure reaction, a manifestation of my carnal self. I am not thinking in terms of "me" or "I," I just am. The second most heavenly times are when I am deep in conversation with such people as yourself, when I *lose* my "self" in thought and in the "other." I'll leave my most heavenly times for the imagination . . .

What I am saying is that the best part of living is simply that—living, experiencing. Richard Rohr calls it the "naked now" and anyone who has paid attention to it probably understands what I am trying to say.[1]

That being said, I will get to the main point of your letter now. "What it means to be human" is perhaps the most important question one can ask. If we could settle the issue, then it seems to me that we are close to figuring out how to enter God's kingdom, because as John Calvin aptly noted in his *Institutes*, "Our wisdom, insofar as it ought to be deemed true and solid wisdom, consists of two parts: the knowledge of God and of ourselves. But as these are connected together by many ties, it is not easy to determine which of the two precedes and gives birth to the other."[2] To put it another way, twelfth-century Sufi mystic Ibn al-Arabi once wrote: "Thou art neither ceasing to be nor still existing. Thou art He, without one of these limitations. Then if thou know thine own existence thus, then thou knowest God; and if not, then not."[3] To know God, then, is to know one's Self, and to know one's Self is to know God.

To be clear, when I think of what it means to be human, I am thinking: *what a human does that nothing else does*. I agree with you and Girard that relationships are crucial in forming a person. I tend to be labeled a Christian—and perhaps I am, really—because I grew up in a Christian family. It is very unlikely that upon being

---

1. Rohr, Richard. *The Naked Now: Learning to See as the Mystics See*. New York: Crossroad, 2009.

2. Calvin, *Institutes*, 15.

3. Al-Arabi, *Whoso Knoweth Himself*, 5.

able to read I would have gravitated toward books on Shintoism, but not impossible I suppose. After all, I've been deeply influenced by Buddhist teachings. I would need to hear more, however, before being satisfied that only humans "do relationships," if that is what you are indeed saying. For example, how do we know that puppies do not imitate the desires of others? But, perhaps you mean something different by "what it means to be human." I look forward to delving deeper into your understanding of this.

For now, let me suppose that self-consciousness is the defining characteristic of a human being. Simply put, while a "lower" animal has simple consciousness and is aware of its surroundings, a human being has self-consciousness. That is to say, she can call herself "I." On top of being aware of their surroundings, the human being is also aware of the "self" as being separate from it. In contrast, as Richard Maurice Bucke points out, it's a simple matter to determine that dogs and other animals do not have self-consciousness: by watching a dog's actions, it is easy to see what is going on in its mind.[4] We know what it sees and hears, and fairly obviously so. If dogs truly did possess self-consciousness, it would have been known long ago. I will leave it at that for now, and await your clarification of what makes humans different than the lower animals.

"May the grace of our Lord Jesus Christ be with your spirit."

~ GALATIANS 6:18

Until next time,

Michael

---

4. Bucke, *Cosmic Consciousness*, 1–2.

Letter 3

A Clarification of Mimetic Desire

Michael,

When differentiating between human beings and the lower animals, you may very well be correct in saying that self-consciousness is at the very heart of the matter. Perhaps that should *really* be our starting place when discussing what it means to be human. Regarding this divine gift, cultural anthropologist Ernest Becker writes:

> Man emerged from the instinctive thoughtless action of the lower animals and came to reflect on his condition. He was given a consciousness of his individuality and his part-divinity in creation, the beauty and uniqueness of his face and his name. At the same time he was given the consciousness of the terror of the world and of his own death and decay.[1]

As an aside, and without getting into any minute details, this is what Becker posits is the reason for such violence in the world—it is this terror we have over death. Because we believe ourselves to be the heroes of the cosmos, so to speak, and because we also have consciousness of our impending doom, we do everything in our

---

1. Becker, *Denial of Death*, 69.

power to defend the systems we create that protect this "immortal self." As philosopher Glenn Hughes notes:

> We have to protect ourselves against the exposure of our absolute truth being just one more morality-denying system among others, which we can only do by insisting that all other absolute truths are false. So we attack and degrade—preferably kill—the adherents of different mortality-denying-absolute-truth systems. So the Protestants kill the Catholics; the Muslims vilify the Christians and vice versa; upholders of the American way of life denounce communism; the Communist Khmer Rouge slaughters all the intellectuals in Cambodia; the Spanish Inquisition tortures heretics; and all good students of the Enlightenment demonize religion as the source of all evil. The list could go on and on.[2]

Anyway, back to the topic at hand.

I believe that both you and Becker are correct in that a very large part of humankind's uniqueness when compared to other animals, is his recognition of "his face and name,"[3] or simply, that he has self-consciousness. That being said, allow me to clarify something so we can then build upon *that* understanding of the human. I will begin by answering the question you posed in your previous letter, "How do we know that puppies do not imitate the desires of others?"

First, we should note that we do witness what seems like mimesis in all forms of life.[4] As Girard explains, "in man's nearest relatives, the anthropoid apes, it [mimesis] manifests itself in some quite spectacular forms."[5] I have noticed this when observing your two energetic dogs, Teddy and Dixie. Whenever you show Teddy affection, for example, your lab, Dixie, always needs your immediate attention as well. I have also witnessed this same jealousy in my little terrier Cocoa, most obviously when I am rough-housing with

2. Hughes, "The Denial of Death and the Practice of Dying," para. 5.
3. Becker, *Denial of Death*, 69.
4. Girard, *Things Hidden*, 90.
5. Ibid.

my daughter Elyse. Sure enough, he always grabs his "buddy" and jumps on both of us, tail wagging like a propeller, playfully growling, and ready to "battle." But what we do not notice is the type of mimetic desire seen in humans; or in other words, desires derived, not from any instinct, but wholly from the perceived desires of another. I will put forth an example to explain.

Let us think about diamonds for a second. Human beings love them. Why? Other than them being "shiny," they really do not offer us anything of sustenance. But we desire them deeply, do we not? We save up for three months just to buy one when we are ready to propose to that special gal (or guy). Then, it is recommended that we purchase more diamonds if we remain married for ten, thirty, sixty, seventy-five, eighty, eighty-five, and ninety years. Talk about obsession! This is, in whole, due to *mimesis*. That is to say, we desire diamonds only because of the simple fact that others desire them.

Focusing our attention back on canines for a moment, I will say that their desires, while in one way mimetic, seem more fixed, or instinctual. Dogs eat, drink, play fetch, compete for belly-scratches, and accost the postal-worker, but they do not desire name brands because of the perceived desires of the other. That would be a rather ridiculous notion.

Building upon this, another vast difference between humanity and the lower animals is in how our societies arise. Again, here is Girard:

> What interests us directly is the role of mimetic conflict in the establishment of animal societies. The individual that cedes first will always cede thereafter; it will yield the first place, the best food, and the females of choice to the victor without dispute. The relationship can be called into question again but generally it maintains a certain stability.[6]

So while non-human animals engage in violence—*sometimes brutally so*[7]—we witness *more* stability within animal groups than in

6. Ibid.

7. For a detailed look at non-human violence, see Melvin Konner's essay,

human societies because of the non-human's ability to concede and remain in concession to the "alpha male" of the group. This is something human beings have a very difficult time doing—as we generally don't agree on whom the alpha male is nor do we allow him to stay at the top very long, so we structure our societies quite dissimilarly. (We'll chat more about this in our first refrain.)

I hope that I was able to elucidate the difference between mimesis in non-human animals and mimesis (specifically with regards to desire) in human ones. Now, I would like to refocus our attention back on this concept of self-consciousness. I am eager to hear what more you have to say with regards to the self-conscious human. What benefits are there? What pitfalls do we find? More pointedly, do you find the notion of self-consciousness to be, like Becker, a bit paradoxical? That is to ask, is it somewhat of a blessing and a curse?

"May the God of hope fill you with all joy and peace in believing, so that you may abound in hope by the power of the Holy Spirit."

~ ROMANS 15:13

I look forward to your response,

Matthew

"Violent Origins: Mimetic Rivalry in Darwinian Evolution," (137–60) in *How we Became Human: Mimetic Theory and the Science of Evolutionary Origins.*

Letter 4

The Pitfalls of Self-Consciousness

Matthew,

Before tackling the subject at hand, I need to redefine something from my first letter, so as to give credit where it is due. You see, if I am anything, really, it is not simply a Christian or a Buddhist, but a Wattsian. I consider myself a student of Alan Watts because, apart from my dad, Watts has had the greatest influence upon my intellectual life. His down-to-earth wisdom is a powerful antidote to all the esoteric nonsense one finds out there—a perfect fit for a lazy-ass like myself. It is safe to assume, then, that everything I say in these letters, unless otherwise stated, can be traced back to his mind in one way or another.

Now, to answer the question from the end of your previous letter, yes, self-consciousness is a curse when it is misused. Allow me to attempt to explain how.

Life in the here and now—the only life we have, really—boils down to what we are aware of, which would include the senses, our thoughts, emotions, etc. Watts likens us to scanning devices that take in life, one snapshot at a time.[1] Over time, we build a database of snapshots that we consciously or non-consciously refer to in order to create a symbol of who we are. We could call this the

---

1. Watts, *Still the Mind*, 48.

ego and there is nothing inherently wrong with it. Like looking at photos from a vacation we have taken, it can be enjoyable to look back at the journey our symbolic self has taken. But no one mistakes a photograph of Mt. Shasta for its totality and no one should mistake our symbolic self for our true self.

At least, no one should!

So, the first potential pitfall of self-consciousness is that it makes it incredibly difficult for us to *fully* know our true self, to know our true identity. Most of us simply fall prey to mistaking the ego for the Self, which is a reality that could not be further from the truth. For example, sometimes we refer to the ego to decide whether or not we will be successful at a task. How many would-be artists fail to create simply because this symbolic self said they could not? So the ego wins and no art gets created. And yet, they are still an artist at heart. (In fact, because creativity is a uniquely human thing, all of us are!) Or, most relevant to our own lives, *how many people have we met who are afraid to have an honest discussion about God and the nature of reality for fear that it will lead to an attack on this symbolic self?* They remain trapped behind a dim glass, never searching, never digging, and assuming what they already know about themselves and about God to be true.

Oh, how the fragility of the ego is so obvious sometimes.

The second potential pitfall of self-consciousness is that we tend to fall in love with it. Like Narcissus, we cannot stop checking in with ourselves. Are we having fun? Are we hurting? Are we pretty? I tentatively suggest, however, that self-consciousness is actually *best* used when we're not directly aware of it. To reiterate something from my previous letter, when I am attempting a difficult hill climb on my dirt bike, I completely lose all sense of "me" as an individual. I know that "I" am on a dirt bike, but what I am directly aware of is the experience of climbing a hill. Not to be crass, but the best love made is while in the present moment, where all attention is given to the partner, and nothing from the past or speculative future is brought into the "naked" now (pardon the pun). I think you might be able to see, then, that the joy of

The Pitfalls of Self-Consciousness

self-consciousness, as Watts puts it, is that it creates a resonance in life.[2] At this point, I cannot improve or elaborate upon that comment. The Buddhist, if you recall, avoids conceptualizing reality, and quite conveniently, I will admit.

Now, back to our discussion on mimesis...

I liked your distinction between human and animal desires, and will take for granted that it is accurate. What I am curious about, of course, is *why* humans desire what the "other" desires. I remember Girard saying that mimetic desire is what makes humans free[3] and I am trying to find a connection—any connection, really—between human mimesis and self-consciousness. Nothing is obvious to me at the moment, and I will not force an answer, but I would like to keep an eye out during our discussions. Part of our camaraderie, as you mentioned earlier, is our shared desire to find connections between apparently disparate ideas.

I look forward to anything and everything that you have to say.

"May the grace of the Lord Jesus be with you."

~ 1 Corinthians 16:23

Live long and prosper,

Michael

---

2. Watts, *Tao of Philosophy*, 8–9.
3. Girard, *I See Satan*, 15.

Letter 5

Positive Mimesis and a Relational God

Michael,

Thank you for your delightful letter. I thoroughly enjoyed reading it, many times over in fact! Here are my initial thoughts.

 First, I love Watts' scanning device analogy, as I believe it is a fitting one. I would, however, add even greater emphasis on the non-conscious nature of this symbolic self you speak of. I think too often—especially in the United States, where autonomy is king—people believe they are essentially islands unto themselves. Sure, we in the West play lip service to the sub and non-conscious, acknowledging how influential we are over one another, but in the end, we still argue tooth and nail that we have both libertarian free will and also *complete* autonomy apart from others. But such isolation—as exposed by the mimetic theory,[1] modern psychology,[2] as well as philosophers such as your dad and Thomas Talbott[3]—only exists as a *façade*.

---

 1. See Girard, *I See Satan*, 15–16.

 2. See Oughourlian, *Genesis of Desire*, 34.

 3. See Machuga, *Three Theological Mistakes*, 173–99, and Talbott, *Inescapable Love of God*, 167–89.

Now, to your point about the true self and the inability to fully know it: while I agree with you that we may never fully understand the true self—or simply, the Self—and while this is quite a pitfall, I must say that ultimately, it is not a bad thing. In fact, it is to be expected, for the Self is that which is made in the very image of the infinite God, so there is always more for our symbolic self to know and understand about *that* part of us. After all, as outwardly infinite as the cosmos is; the temple of the soul is inwardly just as infinite.

That being said, I think it is now an appropriate time to move on to the main point of what I have to say in this letter. For the past few days, I have been kicking around your inquiry into whether there is a connection between self-consciousness and mimesis, as well as your question: "why [do] humans desire what the 'other' desires?" After a lot of thinking, I believe I have come up with something of a worthy response, hopefully one that satisfies your intellectual curiosities.

When Girardians discuss mimesis, it is generally in a negative sense. You will hear us say things like: "mimetic desire leads to rivalry and violence." What we mean is that because we imitate each other's desires, we often find ourselves in rivalry and conflict over something. That is to say, in taking on another as a model, we then become rivals for the one thing we both cannot have (the technical term is "model-obstacle relationship"). This is what Girard calls "scandal."[4] Yet, in spite of this, mimesis can be positive. That is one reason Jesus Christ is such an important figure.

FOLLOW ME

When Jesus gives the command to follow him,[5] he is not doing so in order to simply say "come see what I am doing," but rather, "literally, *follow* what I am doing!" What Jesus is asking others to do is to become *imitators* of him as he is only going to be doing what

---

4. Girard, *I See Satan*, xi–xii.
5. Matt 4:19; 16:24, Mark 1:17; 10:21, Luke 5:27; 18:22, John 1:43; 21:19.

Act I: Exploring the Human

his *non-rivalrous* Father is doing. Because, as pastor Brian Zahnd so frankly points out, "God is like Jesus. God has always been like Jesus. There has never been a time when God was not like Jesus."[6] This is emphasized throughout John's gospel.

- "The Son can do nothing on his own, but only what he sees the Father doing; for whatever the Father does, the Son does likewise. The Father loves the Son and shows him all that he himself is doing." John 5:19–20

- "For I have come down from heaven, not to do my own will, but the will of him who sent me." John 6:38

- "When you have lifted up the Son of Man, then you will realize that I am he, and that I do nothing on my own, but I speak these things as the Father instructed me." John 8:28

- "What my Father has given me is greater than all else, and no one can snatch it out of the Father's hand. The Father and I are one." John 10:29–30

- "I have not spoken on my own, but the Father who sent me has himself given me a commandment about what to say and what to speak." John 12:49

The Father and Son's relationship with each other and then with us acts as a sort of chain—from the Father to Jesus and then from Jesus to us—Jesus reveals both the heart of God as well as what being truly human is all about. And because God steps into humanity through Jesus, the heart of God is reflected in humanity, which Jesus pointedly defines when he refers to himself as "the son of man, who came not to be served but to serve" (Mark 10:45). So, we are to follow in serving others, in giving away ourselves for the other, just as Jesus did, and just as the Father did.[7] Catholic theologian James Alison puts it this way: "The Father wants us to see himself in Jesus so that we may start to build a new humanity

---

6. Zahnd, "God is like Jesus," para. 1.

7. The Greek term for this self-emptying nature of Christ is "kenosis," and is used in Philippians 2:7, "But [Jesus] emptied himself, taking the form of a slave, being born in human likeness."

from the victim, rather than over against victims as we continually do."[8] And when we can live in this way, we can discover the true self, which is made in the image of the Father. That is also where we will discover true peace, or what the Bible refers to as the "kingdom of God."

The key point here is that God made us to desire what the other desires so that God could have relationship with self-conscious beings. He did this by becoming flesh (John 1:14)—*one of us*—to be our model for *positive mimesis*. He did this because he loves us. In fact, God is love (1 John 4:8). And in love, he gives us the ultimate theological-anthropological revelation (Tony Bartlett's term).[9] Without mimesis none of this could happen. Relationship between the divine and humanity would be thwarted.

I hope that answers your question. If not, I am sure we can continue exploring this topic in later letters. But before we move on to Act II, where we will be turning our attention to the topic of salvation, let's come back to something I glossed over in Letter 3, how human societies, being different than that of the lower animals, are specifically structured. This will be important for us to understand, especially when thinking about how one is "saved," or more specifically, what we are saved from—which I have come to realize is first and foremost from ourselves and our fear of death.

"May the peace of God, which surpasses all understanding, guard your heart and your mind in Christ Jesus."

~ PHILIPPIANS 4:7

As always, remain at peace,

Matthew

8. Alison, *Knowing Jesus*, 112.
9. Bartlett, "Isaiah 53," 201.

First Refrain
The Sobering Truth about Culture and Religion

"The peoples of the world do not invent their gods. They deify their victims."[1]

~ René Girard

Matthew: Earlier, we discussed the differences between the behaviors of the "lower animals" with those of human beings, specifically in terms of mimesis. I noted how the "societies" of the lower animals are, in a way, more stable than human ones because of their ability to concede to the alpha male during conflicts. That is not to say that the lower animals are nonviolent—sometimes far from it—but they tend toward nonviolence more often than humans. That is because, when we fight, we do so not only unto death, like the lower animals, but even *after*, as we are also pretty good at taking vengeance upon others in the name of the deceased. If you recall the founding murder myth from the book of Genesis, a slain Abel cries for vengeance from the grave (Gen 4:10). Retributive violence becomes cyclical

---

1. Girard, *I See Satan*, 70.

and, like a flood, begins to wipe out entire civilizations and cultures. That is precisely the point of Genesis 2–11. If you count generations between the slaying of Abel at the hands of Cain, and Lamech's prideful boasting that he takes vengeance "seventy times sevenfold" on children (Gen 4:23–24), you will barely need two hands. It is only a matter of time until the violence spirals out of control and the whole human race—sans Noah and his family—are wiped out.

Michael: It does seem counterintuitive that a species as violent and vengeful as ours could ever live and coexist with each other. Maybe it is a stretch, even, to say that we do, given such atrocities as the Holocaust, the genocide against the Tutsi by the Hutu, and the current Syrian crisis. While in theory human societies are a good thing, it is clear that they, as well as the cultures and religions that follow, are based on something fundamentally flawed. Perhaps you could explain what this something is.

Matthew: Some folks may not want to admit this, but we basically structure our world with the blood of our victims. As Jesus, in Luke 11:49–51, so eloquently put it:

> I will send them prophets and apostles, some of whom they will kill and persecute, so that this generation may be charged with the blood of all the prophets shed *since the foundation of the world*, from the blood of Abel to the blood of Zechariah, who perished between the altar and the sanctuary (emphasis mine).

What Jesus is referring to, of course, is Cain's murder of Abel, as well as the subsequent founding of the city of Enoch. In essence, Jesus is telling us that the world as we know it, with all of its cultural norms, holiness codes, sacrificial mechanisms, economies of exchange—everything that makes a culture a culture, really—are founded and maintained by the blood of a seemingly endless stream of victims.

However, what Jesus is saying here is not anything new. Sure, he prophetically calls it like it is, and foresees the destructive road violence would lead his people down, but well prior to Jesus, even Greek philosopher Heraclitus aptly noticed how the *logos*—that

ACT I: EXPLORING THE HUMAN

is, the structuring principle of reality—was violence and that war was the king of all.[2] So, in a way—whether consciously or non-consciously—we have known about this for a long time. It is evident, moreover, in the many *myths* we tell. The problem, then, is that the truth is generally hidden, a papering over the reality of our victimizing.

One example of this can be found in the Greek myth of Oedipus the King.

Sophocles' tale begins with an oracle that foreshadows how Oedipus will murder his father, who just so happens to be the king of Thebes, and marry his mother, the queen. So like any good parents, they decide to murder young Oedipus. However, Oedipus is rescued by a couple of shepherds of King Polybus and Queen Merope, who then raise young Oedipus as if he were their own.

After a time, Oedipus learns of the oracle, and in thinking that King Polybus and Queen Merope were his true parents, flees for the city of Thebes in order to spare them. On his way, he runs into a stranger and slays him. Whoops, mistake one—*that was his real dad*. Kingless, the city of Thebes becomes held captive by a Sphinx. So here comes Oedipus to the rescue. He solves the riddle, which causes the Sphinx to kill herself thus saving Thebes from captivity. Whoops, mistake two—the recently delivered Thebans make Oedipus their king, which means, you guessed it, that *his mother is made his queen*.

This makes Apollo very angry, so he sends a plague upon the people of Thebes. Tormented, the only thing for them to do is *expel* Oedipus. And when they do, the plague is lifted and peace ensues.

And that, frankly, is the lie of mythology, where the victim is depicted as the cause of the problem, the bringer of plagues, famines, diseases, and so on. Then, when this "problematic other" is expelled from the community, all the citizens become unified and *voila*, catharsis—and the gods are pleased.

---

2. In ancient Greek philosophy, "logos" was a term used to describe the principle that structured the world. It was initially used by a pre-Socratic philosopher named Heraclitus, in which he argues that the Logos is directly attached to war and violence, and that "all things come into being and pass away through strife" (fragments DK22B53 and DK22B80).

First Refrain

This is what we barely seem privy to. When we scapegoat others—that is, when we unify over and against our fellow humans—we get so caught up in the mentality of the mob that we are blinded by our bloodlust. When we finally do slay our victims, we all feel such a sense of relief that we cannot help but think how their death was the will of the gods. Then, this "peace-inducing" event must be repeated so we can stay in right relationship with our gods. Hence, we reenact it, oftentimes by sacrificing our fellow humans, as often as need be, in these "sacred" *rituals*.

Michael: So, that covers two of Girard's "pillars of culture" (*myth* and *ritual*), with the only other one needed for a society to function being *taboo*, correct?

Matthew: Exactly. In fact, prohibitions are most likely the first thing a society attempts as a way of maintaining peace, with rituals and myths following suit. But like the Greek *pharmakon*, prohibitions are both a remedy and a poison. For example, when a guy in high school tells his buddies that he is "going out" with a girl, he is essentially saying that "she is mine, but also not yours." The "she is mine" gesture intensifies his friends' desire for the girl—as our desires are mimetic—while the "not yours" part inflames them even more as we seem to always want what we cannot have. That is to say, prohibitions twist our desires. Just look at Adam and Eve.

This is why the Decalogue's tenth commandment is such a beautiful attempt at getting to the heart of the problem. Exodus 20:17 reads, "You shall not desire your neighbor's house; you shall not desire your neighbor's wife, or male or female slave, or ox, or donkey, or anything that belongs to your neighbor" (my translation). The important thing here to consider is, not the objects in and of themselves, but the fact that their value is infinitely increased by their being possessed by the neighbor. The list could have included anything, really, as long as it belongs to the neighbor (or anyone else we spend time with or associate with). In our modern society, perhaps donkeys and oxen are of little use for most, so we do not need to worry about getting into a mimetic rivalry with our neighbor over them. But his gorgeous new house, 2017 Mercedes-Benz E-Class, brand new pair of jet-skis, and 84" Class Ultra High Definition 3D Smart TV are all things we should probably refrain from fixing our minds on.

Michael: It seems, then, that the expulsion of "the other" has been, on the whole, the peacekeeping strategy of humanity thus far. Or, in other words, culture itself is predicated on scapegoating. We assume our faculties of judgement are infallible, so if something is perceived as dangerous, we kill it. Forget trying to understand it. Forget trying to reconcile or rehabilitate it. Just kill it, and sit back and enjoy the catharsis. Being our resident expert on Christianity, how, then, was Jesus so special? What was his strategy? How does he attempt to preserve the peace?

Matthew: Well, in all reality, Jesus does not preserve the peace. The "preservation of peace" is entirely a human culture thing—peace-*keeping* via taboo and ritualized bloodletting. What Jesus does is open up a whole new way of being, that is to say, the Way of peace-*making* (Matt 5:9). He does this in a number of ways—by employing a non-retributive hermeneutic (Matt 5:38–45; Luke 4:18–30, 7:18–23), by attaching one's love of God to one's love for others (Matt 22:34–40; Luke 10:25–37), and by emphasizing mercy over anything else (Luke 6:36; John 8:1–11)—but what I want to emphasize here is that I believe it must begin with the Resurrection, because without it, the Jesus story no doubt fades into obscurity, and probably rather quickly.

With the Resurrection, however, comes the introduction of the forgiving victim, or what James Alison calls "the intelligence of the victim."[3] Unlike Abel, whose blood cries for vengeance, the blood of the scapegoated Jesus cries for *shalom*, for peace—a vastly superior word indeed (Heb 12:24). This is seen most strikingly in John 20. After appearing to Mary Magdalene, the risen Jesus shows himself to the fearful disciples who are hiding in an upper room, and immediately says "peace be with you" (John 20:19). Bearing

---

3. Alison, *Knowing Jesus*, 32–33.

the scars of his victimage (v. 20), he then repeats himself: "Peace be with you. As the Father has sent me, so I send you" (v. 21). Earlier, we discussed how Jesus only did the will of the Father, and in his doing so, revealed both his true humanity and likewise, a perfect theological framework. The risen Jesus does the same here, releasing the Spirit of forgiveness and shalom (vv. 22–23), which is what the Father is all about, and frankly, has always been about. If you recall, in the gospels God's perfection is described in two ways: enemy love (Matt 5:43–48) and pure mercy (Luke 6:36). This is manifested most profoundly with the eschatological shalom of Christ Jesus, brought about only because of the Resurrection, and is some pretty damn good news, is it not?

Michael: It certainly bears consideration, and it is much better news than the false gospel most Christians espouse. Pardon me, but if Christianity is anything but this, then please count me out.

Matthew: Amen to that.

Michael: One final thing that I am curious about is this—do the Hebrew Scriptures offer us any foreshadowing, or does the peace of Jesus just pop out of nowhere? That is to ask, is there any hinting at a figure such as Jesus found in the Jewish Bible?

Matthew: Absolutely, we find Christ figures all throughout the Hebrew Scriptures—the Suffering Servant of Second Isaiah and the Son of Man from the book of Daniel, for two such examples. One of my favorite stories, though, is the one about Joseph and his brothers from Genesis 37—50. It is here where we find strikingly good news from one of Israel's patriarchs.

The story of Joseph and his brothers reads as a myth. In fact, it parallels the myth of King Oedipus quite brilliantly. And because of this, many discredit it. However, there are key dissimilarities crucial for our consideration.

Like the Oedipus myth, the story of Joseph begins with a prophetic word. In this tale though, the visions come in the form

Act I: Exploring the Human

of Joseph's dreams, which all point to the fact that one day *all* of his brothers would bow down and serve him. This infuriates the brothers so they plot to kill him—just like how Oedipus' parents did when they learned of the oracle. But, like Oedipus, Joseph narrowly escapes.

He is then sold into slavery, deceived, and imprisoned under false pretenses. However, because Joseph has the gift of interpreting dreams, he quickly garners the attention and even affection of the Pharaoh, until one day, Joseph is made Vizier, that is, the Pharaoh's right hand man. At this point, we should note how both tales—that of Oedipus and also this one—attribute the main character's ability to solve/interpret riddles as what leads to their rise in status. For Oedipus, he is made king of Thebes because he solved the riddle of the Sphinx. For Joseph, he becomes Vizier because of his ability to solve the riddle of the Pharaoh's dreams—which prophesied how the land would experience seven years of abundance followed by seven years of famine.

Now, during the time of the famine, Joseph's brothers travel to Egypt to purchase some much needed grain. Long story short: after Joseph deceives the brothers with what seemed like an ill-thought-out plan, he ends the charades and reveals his identity. Yet, he does not do so with anger or malice in his heart, as many of us perhaps would, but instead, with mercy. Finally, after their father Jacob passes away, the story ends with Joseph out and out forgiving his brothers—who feared retribution—for their original treachery, which then causes all of them to fall at Joseph's feet. Thus, the prophecy that they would all serve him becomes fulfilled.

What the story of Joseph teaches is the opposite of myth. Remember, the city of Thebes finds deliverance from the curse *after* they expel a "guilty" Oedipus. The king did the crime, and so had to be sent away, or else the Apollonian plague would no doubt remain. But the Joseph story states the opposite. Joseph is not guilty of anything, the brothers are. But in spite of that the victim offers forgiveness. This is what then brings reconciliation.

Turning our attention to Jesus, notice how the writer of Colossians talks about the reconciliation of all things that Christ brings. In Colossians 1:20, it is said that peace is made through the blood of the cross, where Jesus was emphatic about this: "Father forgive them; for they know not what they are doing" (Luke 23:34). To that end, if God will one day have everyone bow to Christ, as St. Paul so clearly states (see Rom 14:11 and Phil 2:10), I believe it will be in the same way all of Joseph's brothers bowed to Joseph. If not, then I fear the Gospel shares more similarities with mythology than it does with the story of Joseph. What I mean to say is that, myth states peace and reconciliation is at the expense of others (as in Oedipus' expulsion from Thebes), whereas good news brings peace and reconciliation through the forgiveness of others (as in Joseph's forgiveness of his treacherous brothers).

Michael: So, in this quite organic and anthropologic way, we could agree with the writer of 2 Timothy 3:16 and say that the Scriptures are "inspired/God-breathed," in that in their teaching, they address, at least in some places, this papering over of the lie of myth that you spoke of earlier?

Matthew: Without getting into the grammar of that passage or what is meant by the term *theópneustos* (God-breathed), yes, I tend to think that is the case.

Michael: It seems much more plausible than claiming 2 Timothy 3:16 means that the Bible is the inerrant and/or infallible word of God. Talk about a non-sequitur! If anything, a set of Scriptures, in order to be considered "inspired by God," better address humanity's seemingly dire situation. And inerrancy fails to do this. That is how I see it anyway.

Matthew: Again, I would have to agree with you there. Inerrancy is, in the grand scheme of things, a rather recent idea—largely a Protestant response to the issue of Papal authority. *If the Bible can be made authoritative—if it is inerrant and infallible—no one, not even the Pope, can tell us what it says.* So now, nearly five-hundred years later, what you have are countless Protestant Popes, all asserting that biblical literalism is the preferred exegetical method to approach the Bible with.

Michael: It is a sad state of affairs we find ourselves in, is it not? But we shall press on, and I am convinced folks like you will continue to lead others from the outdated and if I may be frank, dreadfully boring notion of *sola scriptura*. May the grace of Christ Jesus be with you (Phil 4:23).

Matthew: And with you. Shalom.

ACT II

Exploring Salvation

Letter 6

Heaven is At-Hand

Dear Matthew,

Coming from an Eastern mouth, salvation can be a misleading word to the Western mind. Based on how I understand things, the Eastern religions tend to assume a reality that is essentially safe, one where the soul is never in danger of being obliterated or tortured for time-everlasting. At least, this seems to be how the enlightened within these faith traditions think of things. As Fr. Richard Rohr writes:

> The people who know God well—the mystics, the hermits, those who risk everything to find God—always meet a lover, not a dictator. God is never found to be an abusive father or a tyrannical mother, but always a lover who is more than we dared hope for. How different than the "accounting manager" that most people seem to worship. God is a lover who receives and forgives everything.[1]

That is simply to say, everything is all good—nothing to worry about here![2]

---

1. Rohr, *Everything Belongs*, 131.
2. See Matthew 6:25.

There is, however, a journey of the soul. And if the soul continues to act in a way that is unbefitting of the heavenly life, then it will remain in this life of "death and sorrow." But, nirvana is always there, waiting for the soul to be ready. And the soul that gets there *first* is no more valuable than the soul that gets there *last*. Jesus teaches something like this in the Parable of the Laborers (Matt 20:1–16). The worker who begins work in the vineyard at nine o'clock gets paid the same wage as those who start at noon, three, and five o'clock. No more, no less.

The fact is this: we are in no way obliged to assume the high-stakes-game that some forms of Christianity assume. As I mentioned in my introduction, for me, it took the form of Arminianism. Many of this ilk tend to think that if the soul does not have to make a decision of gigantic importance, then life and love are somehow reduced. *If there is no hell, then what is the point?* one may rhetorically ask. But is this dualistic ending to the human drama where life and love get their value? As if life and love are found in proving one's self right, while those who are wrong suffer eternal death. No! Life and love are self-evidently good—we need no eternal ultimatum to see this.

Any religion worth your time will tell you that heaven is at-hand, for in the heavenly life, you will not be constantly trying to get to heaven; as if heaven was something you travel upward toward. In other words, you will not have to climb Jacob's ladder to get there (see Gen 28:10–19). So, "Wake up!" and realize that life is in the living—which I find illustrated most beautifully in the following Jewish prayer:

> *How Wonderful, O Lord, are the works of your hands!*
> *The heavens declare your glory,*
> *The arch of the sky displays your handiwork*
> *In your love you have given us the power*
> *To behold the beauty of your world*
> *Robed in all its splendor.*
> *The sun and the stars, the valleys and the hills,*
> *The rivers and the lakes all disclose your presence.*

The roaring breakers of the sea tell of your awesome might,
The beast of the field and the birds of the air
Bespeak your wondrous will.
In your goodness you have made us able to hear
The music of the world. The voices of the loved ones
Reveal to us that you are in our midst.
A divine voice sings through all creation.[3]

Awake to this! It's here, and it's now. And it's quite exquisite.

Perhaps this is my laziness speaking, but it is this now-oriented way of thinking that leads me to believe that there is never really a sense of urgency when thinking about salvation. We'll all get there, and the soul will grow at its own pace, thank you very much. Anything that is rushed is of inferior quality, or, in some cases, actually ruined. No one is foolish enough to think, for example, that pulling on a corn stalk to make it grow faster will do any good. But sure enough, it happens. I fear that huge swaths of religious people—the so-called pious and moral—are not being ushered into heaven, then, but hastened into hell by the impetus we call religion.

Before I close, I want to qualify all of this and say that I still think salvation *can be* an appropriate word *in a certain context*, just not the context of something like an eternal torture chamber called hell. I would never want to downplay the woes of this world or suggest that heaven, either in the present reality or the posthumous speculative, fails in being massively better than how things are, on the whole, at the present moment for most people. From the looks of things, humanity needs saving from something—perhaps from our very selves and our violent mechanisms. And this saving is the *prize* that we are all striving for, is it not?

I never tire of speculating about heaven. I think it is healthy. If we are truly made in the image of God—that is, if everyone has the spark of the divine—I think honest speculation will naturally

---

3. This prayer, entitled "How Wonderful, O Lord," can be found at http://www.worldhealingprayers.com/7.html.

Act II: Exploring Salvation

reveal truth. So what of it, my friend? What excites you about God and more specifically, salvation and "heaven?"

"May the grace of the Lord Jesus Christ be with your spirit."
~ Philemon 25

Salaam,

Michael

Letter 7

A Changing Understanding of What It Means to Be Saved

Michael,

I believe you are quite correct that "honest speculation will naturally reveal truth." At least, I hope that is how God set things up. And I do think that is why Jesus does some tinkering with the Torah's command about how to love God. Notice the difference between the following:

- Deut 6:5: "You shall love the Lord your God with all your heart, and with all your soul, and with all your might."
- Matt 22:37: "You shall love the Lord your God with all your heart, and with all your soul, and with *all your mind*." (emphasis mine)

It is pretty clear: we have to think about things! So it stands to reason that if we earnestly and rationally seek the Source from which we are derived—using the mind the Creator gave us—then we *will* discover God.[1]

---

1. What I am not saying is that we will be able to know everything about God, or have a perfect theological framework. Rather, I am saying that we can discover the Father's true nature, as he has been fully revealed (in human form) in Christ Jesus. However, like an onion, the more you peel back the

Act II: Exploring Salvation

The more I have used my mind to think about God, the more excited I have become about such things as salvation. After all, when anyone, after years of sojourning, concludes that God is wholly merciful, wholly loving, and wholly gracious, how could they not be excited when it comes to thinking about heaven, both in the here and now and on into the forever?

But, as you are well aware, I was not always so jazzed about this topic.

Like you, I grew up an Arminian. I no doubt accepted the "common" spiel: "ask Jesus to 'come into your heart' and you will be saved." This *economy of exchange* model of soteriology made sense on one level—offer something to God and receive blessing (see Deut 28)—but believing God *really* behaved this way was actually quite terrifying. That is because many of my friends were a "them," or in other words, non-Christian, including a good friend who died in a traffic accident during my teenage years. What was God going to do to *him*? I dare not imagine! Furthermore, thinking selfishly for a moment, I did not always exactly behave like an "us"—just check my internet browser history during my high school years, most notably.[2] Would I, the center of my own cosmos, not have made the cut?

So, salvation in the sense where we are *potentially* saved from God's own design was not a very exciting matter. The Christianity I knew definitely did not seem worthy of being labeled *euangelion* (good news) but rather, something more fitting would have been *dysangelion* (bad news). Thus, when something worthy of being called "good news" was sought after, I found this dualistic model to be, as I deep down suspected, vastly wanting.

My previous beliefs had very little to say about the kingdom of God being "at hand." What I essentially believed about God's kingdom was that it was all about securing my best self-interests for the afterlife. Specifically, I wanted to be included in the Rapture,

---

layers of a fully revealed God, the more you discover and thus, the more you peel. Thus, it is quite cyclical and even, quite paradoxical.

2. If you didn't get that joke, it means that I looked at a lot of porn. Sorry mom.

lest I found myself left behind with the rest of the reprobates. Like you mentioned earlier, if our faith tradition has little to say about the here and now, focusing instead on the there and then, then it probably is not worth having. Jürgen Moltmann puts it this way: "The notion that this life is no more than a preparation for a life beyond, is the theory of a refusal to live, and a religious fraud."[3] And none of this stuff—premillenial dispensationalism, a dualistic eschatology, etc.—was worth having! Not by a long shot.

Probing deeper, my former understanding of Christianity had nothing to say about what we are truly saved from, namely, the *powers* and *principalities* that structure our often fucked-up world. In fact, in typical Western models of the atonement, it takes most of the blame off of humanity and places it onto God, unabashedly boasting that Jesus stepped in between us and God's terrible fury. I know I am hyperbolizing things, but that sounds like an older brother who steps in front of his again drunk dad, who is about to haul off and beat the living hell out of you, the youngest sibling. But because big bro Jesus is such a swell guy, he takes the pummeling instead.

Apologies must go out to the Calvinists out there if I no longer find anything of value with that model, for it seems nothing more than psychological projection.

Now that I believe differently, however, I love talking about God, because through God, as modeled by the son Jesus—the Great Physician—we find true healing. In fact, *sózó*, the Greek verb translated "salvation," carries with it the context of being healed, or preserved. This salvation, though, is not salvation from a divine Abu Ghraib, or from a "divine child abuser,"[4] but salvation from ourselves and our plight. That is to say, it is salvation from our satanic systems of power and our fear of death—as well as our own ego! It is salvation that states "have trust that you can live truly human, giving one's self away to the other just as the son of man did,

---

3. Moltmann, *Coming of God*, 50.

4. See Anthony Bartlett's essay "Atonement: Birth of a New Humanity" in *Stricken by God?* for a brief survey of feminist theologians who have argued that penal substitution atonement theory is in fact "divine child abuse."

and if you do, you will be saved from everything that holds you back from the kingdom of God." Like you said—and Jesus too—*the kingdom of God is at-hand*. And what better way to experience this than to hold fast to the idea that not even death holds us back from renouncing our "self," and from freely giving our love and grace and forgiveness to everyone, even our enemies. As Krishna teaches Arjuna in *The Bhagavad Gita*: "They are forever free who renounce all selfish desires and break away from the ego-cage of 'I,' 'me,' and 'mine' to be united with the Lord. This is the supreme state. Attain this, and pass from death to immortality."[5]

If we can do this, have we not tasted what the kingdom of God is *like*?

I think we have.

I believe I am at a good place, then, to turn it back to you. I will conclude by playing a bit of "devil's advocate," posing the question: "Do you need to '*believe*' in Jesus in order to be saved (i.e., 'go to heaven')?" Is that not what many Christians are going to no doubt ask, should they be perusing through these pages? Don't most Christians put more emphasis on their belief *about* Jesus than anything else? Isn't the "sin" that keeps people out of the pearly gates the unbelief in Jesus as "personal Lord and savior?" This has been my experience, at least, more often than not. So, what of that retort?

"O give thanks to the Lord, for he is good, for his steadfast love endures forever."

~ PSALM 136:1

May the grace of Christ Jesus comfort you,

Matthew

5. Easwaran, *Bhagavad Gita*, 97.

Letter 8

Sin, Salvation, and Belief in Jesus

Matthew,

Thanks for throwing me under the bus with that question, ya bastard! (I only kid.) But seriously, "Does an individual need to believe in Jesus in order to be saved?" can be one of the more divisive questions that could be asked of a person, yet I shall not shy away.

So let's start by defining our terms, and first up, *belief*.

Belief implies wiggle room. It means having confidence in the truth without having absolute proof. As Watts teaches, "To have faith is to trust yourself to the water. When you swim you don't grab hold of the water, because if you do you will sink and drown. Instead you relax, and float."[1] Let me illustrate the realm of belief by contrasting two statements.

1. God is love
2. 2 + 2 = 4

The first statement, even I will admit, is open for debate, as it falls into the belief category. I believe or trust it to be true, but it does not present itself in the way that objectivity presents itself, in the way that statement two does. It is possible to look at all the pain, suffering, and evil in the world and conclude that God is *not* love.

---

1. Watts, *Essence of Alan Watts*, 37.

Act II: Exploring Salvation

As the famous question goes, "How can an all-powerful, all-good God allow so much evil in the world?" But, in contrast, I could *only* be mistaken about the truth of statement two if my senses have completely failed me, and if logic itself is completely and utterly useless—where 2 + 2 = 5, or some such absurd nonsense.

So that is a primer on *belief*.

Next up: *sin*.

You have mentioned around the bonfire, and I would heartily agree, that sin is best described, not so much as "missing the mark," or breaking God's laws, as is often said, but as more of an attack on relationship—either with God or a fellow human. Calvinist theologian Cornelius Plantinga's explanation is a fabulous one:

> Sin is disruption of created harmony and then resistance to divine restoration of that harmony . . . God hates sin not just because it violates his law but, more substantively, because it violates shalom, because it breaks the peace, because it interferes with the way things are supposed to be. (Indeed, that is why God has laws against a good deal of sin.) God is for shalom and therefore against sin.[2]

The most egregious sin, then, is direct violence against a fellow human. It is the violation of shalom in the most overt way. I do not know any other way of looking at sin without denying the goodness and interconnectedness of creation that we see in the first narrative in Genesis. God's creation is "very good" (Gen 1:31), so any violence against it makes no sense, given that humanity is made in the image of a "very good" God (Gen 1:27).

So, considering the question from your previous letter, depending on how you interpret "believing in Jesus," I am not certain what difference this believing makes to *salvation from sin*, as I understand it. Salvation, we must remember, is a saving from our sin, primarily the sin of violence, not saving from God.

Like believing in Santa Claus, I *previously* understood belief to mean a simple acknowledgement of Jesus' existence—and that he is who he said he is—and so, heaven became an exclusive night

---

2. Plantinga, *Not the Way*, 5.

Sin, Salvation, and Belief in Jesus

club that no one could enter without speaking the magical name of Jesus. But again, how is this effectual in overcoming sin? It might be the first step towards salvation, for some that is, but it cannot be the last.

You could also interpret "believing in Jesus" as believing that what he taught is accurate. Jesus had much to say about loving and forgiving your enemy, and I believe union with God requires these things. How could it not? If I reject my enemy, I am rejecting God in my enemy. Dietrich Bonhoeffer puts it this way: "God loves our enemies—this is what the cross tells us. God suffers for their sake, experiences misery and pain for their sake; the Father has given his dear Son for them. Everything depends on this: that whenever we meet an enemy, we immediately think: this is someone whom God loves; God has given everything for this person."[3] One could say that Jesus indeed saves us from something by modeling this love for us—as Bonhoeffer so eloquently does—but a Buddhist might ask, "What is wrong with our prophets? Why do we need your Jesus to help us with this?" When many in the Buddhist tradition loathe even killing an inchworm, it would seem that they have much to teach us on the matter of enemy love. So, the question is raised: *Can a Buddhist not follow Christ just as well as a Christian, even if she does not happen to have the "correct" language*?

Finally, "believing in Jesus" could mean trusting that he has the power to do what he said he would do. *Christus Victor* is quite possibly my favorite of the atonement theories. It states that Christ defeated Satan, sin, and death. Not me, but Christ. The story goes something like this:

> Satan has enslaved humanity with the fear of death (Heb 2:14–15). All manners of evil arise from this bondage. But Christ comes to set humanity free from Satan's power, that is, "to destroy the devil's work" (1 Pet 5:8). He does so by enduring the cross and by then being raised to life by God (Acts 2:23–25). In doing so, Christ "disarmed the rulers and authorities, exposing them to public disgrace by leading them in a triumphal parade" (Col 2:15).

---

3. Bonhoeffer, *Collected Sermons*, 196.

Act II: Exploring Salvation

> Christ is made Lord (Rom 14:11; Phil 2:11), given the Name above all names (Phil 2:9), and will reign until death, the last enemy, is destroyed (1 Cor 15:24–26). Death will then be cast into the lake of fire (Rev 20:10, 14) so that "God may be all in all" (1 Cor 15:28).

Now, I am fully open to the idea of Jesus—or perhaps, this Cosmic Christ—working with me, and everyone for that matter, in some mysterious way, to defeat sin. The question is, do we have to be consciously aware of this process, or does it work on its own, like chemicals in our bodies? Given that Christians are no better at leading an ethical life than Buddhists, or other various faith traditions for that matter, thus offering evidence that this conscious awareness seems experientially meaningless, I would have to assume the latter.

Ultimately though, who cares about my stance on such an abstraction? Although my belief is important to an extent (as in my logical mind requires comprehension of some key things), it is not the primary thing that aids me in fully engaging the present moment nor does it change how I am going to interact with my neighbor. If I believed that human life was not valuable, the cure to such a thing does not come from an opposing, equally flimsy belief, it comes from the unmistakable potency of the present moment. Belief is subservient to reality, not the other way around. Everything that is truly important in life has been made graciously and gloriously self-evident—love, friendship, companionship, etc. I do not need belief of any kind, for example, to see that my wife is lovely and deserves adoration. Being present with her is all the "proof" needed.

Hopefully, none of what I have said is divisive. It should not be. It should be obvious that the heavenly life is not accomplished when it is *believed*, but when it is *done*. Salvation does not come from subscribing to a set of beliefs *about* Jesus. It does not even come from believing that you should turn the other cheek (once pointed out, the only appropriate response is "duh!"). It comes from the God-given courage to actually do it.

Sin, Salvation, and Belief in Jesus

"The Lord shall preserve thee from all evil: he shall preserve thy soul.

The Lord shall preserve thy going out and they coming in from this time forth, and even for evermore."

~ Psalm 121:7–8 KJV

Be well,

Michael

Letter 9

Jesus is Lord, Period!

Michael,

Thank you for your letter. I was incredibly moved by the depth of that response. It was not half-assed in any way, unlike the rest of your writings. (I only kid.)

Yet sadly, at the end of the day, I am afraid most Christians will miss the power of your words and insist that one must declare "Jesus is Lord" in this life in order to be saved. Of course, this phrase then gets dwindled down to some pint-sized version of its former self, coming to mean nothing more than "Jesus is lord of my life." And so, because this seems to be the reality within Western Christianity (broadly speaking), that is what I am going to talk about in this letter.

What does it really mean for Jesus to be Lord?

First off, this was a very politically charged statement during the first few centuries after Christ. Caesar, at least in the eyes of the Romans, was lord over everyone and everything. He established this through war and conquest, the world being his perpetual battlefield. After the Resurrection of Jesus, though, a rag-tag group of followers began to subversively declare Jesus as Lord over all. And because Caesar's reign was believed to be over all, this was *quite* a statement, because all meant all. Thus, Jesus' lordship was over even Caesar himself, a corporate lordship in the most inclusive of ways.

With that proper historical context in mind, allow me to point to what the Apostle Paul had to say about the phrase "Jesus is Lord."

On two separate occasions, namely Romans 14:11 and Philippians 2:10–11, Paul writes that *all* will declare "Jesus is Lord." Furthermore, they will do so while bowing their knees to Christ. No Christian denies this, at least none that I know of. Of course, they would then go on to say that those who bow and confess last (i.e., unbelievers who die without first saying the magic phrase), will do so as if defeated soldiers on a battlefield. Or, one could say, they will bow and confess in the same way people bowed and confessed to Caesar—begrudgingly or under compulsion. But that is the gospel according to Caesar, not of our Lord Jesus Christ.

Now, because I do not buy the stock line that some will bow and confess in an act of reluctance, like those who bow to petty tyrants, here is what I believe is the real reason for the universality of humanity's confession.

What we must first realize is that as Lord, Jesus is the only rightful judge of the living and the dead (1 Tim 4:2). And the reason is because of what we witnessed at the cross. So, we can never separate who the risen Christ is from who the first-century Jesus of Nazareth was. In terms of character, there is no difference before and after death. We see this most notably when comparing the dying Jesus in Luke 23:34 and the risen Christ in John 20:19–23. Peace and forgiveness pervades in both places.

With Jesus as our most merciful judge, how then should we approach Paul's declaration that all will bow and confess Jesus as Lord? Paul himself informs us how, and does so in two ways. First, in Romans 14:11, he uses the Greek verb *exomologeó*, which not only implies confession but also "giving praise." And so, in the NRSV, the text reads: "Every knee shall bow to me, and every tongue shall *give praise* to God." (emphasis mine) Thus, when all confess that "Jesus is Lord"—whether in this life or in the posthumous—according to Paul, they will be doing so with a grateful heart. They will be praising God! And why wouldn't they? After all, an all-merciful judge is a good thing, is it not? I hardly think they will praise God and then, in spite of this, be roasted for time-everlasting, or annihilated altogether. Quite the contrary, in fact, as, according to Clement of Alexandria:

> It is clear that those who were . . . actually in Hades and "in prison," on hearing the voice of the Lord—either his own voice or that which operated through the Apostles—were converted and believed. For we remember that the Lord is 'the power of God;" and power could never be powerless.
>
> Thus, I fancy, the goodness of God is proved, and the power of the Lord, to save with justice and equity displayed to those who turn to him, whether here or elsewhere. For the energizing power does not come only on men here; it is operative in all places and at all times.[1]

In 1 Corinthians 12:3, Paul also states that "no one can say 'Jesus is Lord' except by the Holy Spirit." So, it raises the question: *If no one can declare "Jesus is Lord" except by the Holy Spirit, and all will eventually do this, will all declarations not be directly because of the Holy Spirit?* Hence, could we not say that God will, through the power of the Holy Spirit, bring all people to openly give praise to God, while *freely* bowing their knees to Jesus? On September 19, 2016, I put it out to my Facebook friends like this:

> The Bible *clearly* states:
>
> > No one can say, "Jesus is Lord," except by the Holy Spirit (1 Cor 12:3).
> >
> > ~ And ~
> >
> > Every tongue will confess that Jesus is Lord (Phil 2:11).
>
> Now, you draw the conclusion.[2]

I think this parallels with what you said in your previous letter, when you stated: "I am fully open to the idea of Jesus—or perhaps, this Cosmic Christ—working with me, in some mysterious

---

1. Clement, *Stromateis*, VI. vi, (47), from Bettenson, *Early Christian Fathers*, 176.

2. https://www.facebook.com/matthew.distefano.7/posts/948397905282522.

way, to defeat sin." In the same way, I am fully open to the idea of the Holy Spirit working with everyone, in some mysterious way, until they give praise to God and declare Jesus as Lord. But this will not be some "coerced" acknowledgment, since it will be the Christ in us (John 1:1–5)—or, in other words, *our true identity*—that freely chooses God in the end. That is the very point of free will—*having the freedom to do the good.*

When it is all said and done, if you must declare Jesus as Lord in order to be saved, in order to be restored and healed, then I cannot think salvation fails to come to anyone, as all will do this under their own free will, through the power of the Holy Spirit. And by the way, I do think you are apt in your assessment of things. For, I must ask: What must "non-believers" such as the very Christlike Gandhi, or Sufi mystic Rumi, be saved *from*? Surely, not the Father of Jesus! Are they (and in fact everyone) not also included in Christ's redeeming work on the cross? Well, if I am, they are. Or, to take Danish philosopher Søren Kierkegaard's approach: "If others are going to hell, then I am going with them. But I do not believe that; on the contrary, I believe that we will all be saved."[3]

Now, before we hear why you personally hold to the doctrine of universal reconciliation, please allow me to end with another quote from Clement, as it not only succinctly sums up everything I have been saying in this letter, but also gives us something mull over in our mind. Regarding Christ's lordship, he asks: "All men are Christ's, some by knowing him, the rest not yet. He is the Savior, not of some and the rest not. *For how is he Savior and Lord, if not the Savior and Lord of all?* (emphasis mine)"[4]

Selah.

Your brother in Christ,

Matthew

3. Kierkegaard, *Journals and Papers*, 557.

4. This quote can be found at http://www.tentmaker.org/Quotes/church-fathersquotes.htm.

Letter 10

Why I am a Universalist

Matthew,

What a beautiful, lucid exposition of what it means when we say "Jesus is Lord." I would have nothing to add or subtract from your letter, only to say how unfortunate it is that most of our interlocutors have entirely missed the point of this powerful declaration. But hopefully, because of folks like you, the times are a-changing.[1]

As you mentioned, we will conclude this collection by answering the question "Why do I hold to the doctrine of universal reconciliation?"

To begin, no one should claim to have deductive certainty about their beliefs. An introductory course in logic shows this (Google "affirming the consequent," for starters). This is not to say that Universalism fails in making a strong case for itself. (Its case is so strong, in fact, that one really has to wonder how people so *readily* come to other conclusions, and most of the time *dogmatically* so.) What it essentially boils down to—and I am oversimplifying things as well as putting faith in both premises—is that if God wants to save everyone and can, then God will. Outside of that, I will not really put forth much of a deeper *logic-and-reason-based* argument at this time, because there is simply not enough space

1. To paraphrase the great poet Bob Dylan.

to treat the subject with respect. Instead, I will refer those seeking a more in-depth discussion of the topic to two books that have helped me. Thomas Talbott's *The Inescapable Love of God* is a great place to start for those interested in heavier philosophical matters. Or, for a gentler introduction, check out Rob Bell's infamous *Love Wins* (just make sure your fundamentalist friends don't find out).

Although my Universalism is partially based on logic and reason, I must again say that it is also based on a simple inability to worship a God that is not perfectly loving and gracious *as well as* able to do what he sets out to do. If I may be frank, I no longer have awe for a God that either cannot save all (Arminianism) or will not save all (Calvinism) of creation. And so, both Arminianism and Calvinism are necessarily hopeless, and, as Christian theologian Jürgen Moltmann notes, being "Without hope is like no longer living. Hell is hopelessness, and it is not for nothing that at the entrance to Dante's hell there stands the words: 'Abandon hope, all ye who enter here.'"[2] So, I have had to make my peace with the fact that if God does not happen to be as loving and gracious as I hope him to be, or if he cannot or will not reconcile all my loved ones—which, per Jesus, includes even my enemies—then, short of complete coercion, there will be no heaven to be had for me, never a time where my tears are forever wiped from my face (Rev 21:4). At least, that seems to be the case as I understand it.

Talking about matters in Buddhist language may take some getting used to for many in the West, but there is this lovely law of "Least Effort," which states that more is accomplished by putting in less effort. For instance, in order to properly taste food, you simply place food on your tongue.[3] The ears do not try to hear, they simply receive sound waves, and squinting only distorts your vision. As Alan Watts notes, "muddy water is best cleared by leaving it alone."[4] Speaking as a writer—and I think you have had the same experience—my greatest insights seem to come out of nowhere, when I have stopped treating the subject at hand as be-

2. Moltmann, *Theology of Hope*, 20.
3. Watts, *Way of Zen*, 19.
4. Ibid., 155.

ing problematic. If you take for granted, then, that effort is utterly contrary to the spirit of heavenly life, or salvation for that matter, then it makes no sense to me that effort would be the mechanism for either. In other words, grasping at heaven is pointless, and is actually only useful to the extent that it shows itself to be useless. To put it back in Christian terms: it is by grace alone, and not by any works that we have been saved (Eph 2:8).

So, if heaven cannot be had by trying to get there, by doing good works, by building our spiritual muscles through painful exercise, so to speak, it seems a matter of justice that God—the Hound of Heaven, the Author and Finisher of our faith—does it for us. Perhaps all we need to do is open our eyes to that reality, or perhaps, as Saul of Tarsus experienced, he will even do *that* for us. And, to answer Swiss theologian Hans Urs von Balthasar's famous rhetorical question "Dare we hope that all men be saved?"[5] Yes, *we dare hope that.*

Does anyone really want the situation to be contrary to this? Isn't everyone tired of all this sweat and toil? I am! I have been warned by several people not to make a god of my own design, and to a degree, that is a very fair warning. God will be God no matter what I think. But if it just so happens that biblical, philosophical, and historical evidence points to Universalism (and I believe they do), and if the most enlightened among other faith traditions seem to be saying essentially the same thing (and many do), why would I *not* embrace such a beautiful vision, and how could God fault me for doing so? But, if God does not happen to be like this, at least my conscience will be clear while I am burning in hell, eh?

I know you are aware that I say "burning in hell" jokingly. Neither of us read the biblical descriptions of hell to mean eternal torment, but both of us believe that a hell of some sort is a definite reality. So, that is what I think we should explore in the following act. But first, let's revisit our earlier conversation on belief. I feel as if more could be said on the matter.

---

5. The work I am referring to is Hans Urs von Balthasar's *Dare we Hope "That All May Be Saved"? With a Short Discourse on Hell*, translated by David Kipp and Lothar Krauth. San Francisco: Ignatius, 1988.

"May the God of hope fill you will all joy and peace in believing, so that you may abound in hope by the power of the Holy Spirit."

~ Romans 15:13

Namaste,

Michael

Second Refrain

In Spite of Everything, Belief Still Matters

"Men never do evil so completely and cheerfully as when they do it from religious conviction."[1]

~ BLAISE PASCAL

Matthew: Earlier, I tossed a very difficult inquiry in your direction. I can admit that. But I think you answered the question "do you need to believe in Jesus in order to be saved?" admirably and thoroughly, while at the same time leaving room for others to further explore and expand upon their own answers.

That being said, as you previously suggested, while belief may not be the primary thing that aids you in fully engaging the present moment, or entering into the kingdom of heaven, it is important, because what we believe about reality does shape how we experience said reality. Does it not?

Michael: Absolutely. Correct belief is important, not because it is a test to be passed, but because it *helps* determine our actions. The

---

1. Pascal, *Pensées*, #894.

logic is simple. I think it is safe to say that regardless the religion or depth of understanding, every theist agrees that God is the ultimate power in the universe. It only makes sense to act in accordance with such a power. So, if I believe that God is love, for instance, I will act lovingly, and I will enter into the kingdom of heaven in the here and now. If I believe God is violent, I'll likely act violently to get what I and (my understanding of) God wants—one could call this being zealous for God—and will enter the kingdom of hell. If you need an analogy for this, think of Paul and Saul—one man, two entirely different theological orientations and then subsequently two starkly dissimilar views of what is considered "ethical."

Matthew: That is just it. Humans are so mimetic, are we not? Simply look around; it is obvious that many of us are using our beliefs in an exclusivist God to justify conflict with others. Should we call that being "Sauline?" We seem to think that it is within our right to bring hell into others' lives, primarily through war, racism, sexism, scapegoating, and greed. All over beliefs! It seems obvious then, that the only beliefs worth having must holistically fit with what we experience in the lovingly peaceful kingdom of heaven. They certainly mustn't contradict it.

The beliefs that *do* are witnessed in the most obvious ways. I make mention of something to this effect in *From the Blood of Abel*:

> Just notice how it is the most rigidly fundamentalist of folks who commit acts of violence in their immortality system's name. It is not the mystical Sufi who straps a bomb to his torso, blowing up hundreds of people. It is the fundamentalist Muslim who does this in the name of Allah. It is not the Franciscan Father who praises the Westboro Baptist Church prior to shooting up a black congregation. It is the fundamentalist Christian who does this in the name of Jesus. It is not the Buddhist monk who shoots the world's most famous Hindu peace activist. It is the member of the fundamentalist Hindu Mahasabha (Hindu nationalist political party in India). And on and on it goes. Many of the people listed above,

and then some who are not, feel that the defending of their ideology and position is a matter of life and death—sadly, often literally so.[2]

Indeed, beliefs lead to real-world problems. Our bad theologies, harmful doctrinal statements, and subsequent piss-poor ethics have really made a mess of things, have they not? Take, for instance, the belief in dispensationalism—or what Michael Hardin hilariously calls "pseudo-speculative theological bullshit"[3]—a doctrinal system we both grew up in. If you don't mind, I am going to pick on this belief system for a moment.

What is so scary about dispensationalism is that it is largely (but not entirely) based on a highly *literal* reading of the book of Revelation—you know, the one chock-full of multi-headed, multi-horned mythological creatures, bowls of wrath, trumpets of apocalypse, bloody war, a winepress of fury, a lake of fire, and then finally a victorious lamb who ushers in the kingdom of heaven. This literalist reading is reflected in the popular *Left Behind* series of books and movies, which essentially state:

> Believers will be raptured into heaven. Then, God's wrath and fury will be unleashed on the earth. Billions will be killed. They will then be thrown into hell, to suffer forevermore. All this will not only be endorsed by Jesus, but he will be the one leading the charge. Believers will rejoice. Hallelujah! *Amen.*

Scary stuff, am I right?

But, notice the first part in particular—believers *will be raptured into heaven*, whisked off to be with Jesus just in the nick of time.

How convenient! Or, as the Church Lady from *Saturday Night Live* would say, "Well, isn't that special?"

Sadly, this (mis)understanding of Christian eschatology has the potential to create not only complete and utter apathy, but something far worse. Sure, there seems to be apathy for the

---

2. Distefano, *Blood of Abel*, 86–87.
3. Hardin, *Walking with Grandfather*, 133.

Second Refrain

environment, and apathy for humanity—and why not, Christians will be out of here!—but, like a double-edged sword, also a promulgation of the very thing these same Christians believe *must take place* before the end can come, before they can go to their party in the sky. This has resulted in attitudes like this one, from conservative commentator Ann Coulter: "God gave us the earth. We have dominion over the plants, the animals, the trees. God said, 'Earth is yours. Take it. Rape it. It's yours.'"[4]

Pardon me while I vomit.

This mindset, which I will admit, is not simply contained within dispensationalism, or even Christianity for that matter, has, not surprisingly, indeed led to a raping of the earth, a raping of the people of the earth, and a raping that continues and will seemingly keep continuing until the end—*because it's simply God's ways*. But herein lies the irony about all this: it seems to all be coming true as a sort of self-fulfilled prophecy, with many in the church loudly and prominently playing right along with this misguided theology, without so much as a clue that they are, quite frankly, an anti-Christ.

There, I said it.

But it's true.

That is why dispensationalism—and similar beliefs—are so dangerous. Because the earth must be consumed in fire, any peace is a false peace (see Dan 9:27). So, in real time and space, peace gets violently sabotaged at nearly every turn. And because violence is cyclical, it keeps escalating and escalating, mimetically, like a faulty pressure-cooker.

And speaking of "mimetic," not only do Christians of this ilk believe this is how the story ends, but so do many fundamentalist Muslims, and even many Jews:

- *Some* Muslims believe that in order for the Madhi (the redeemer of Islam) to return, he must be preceded by violence, war, and intensified *fitnas* (times of trial, affliction, and

---

4. Coulter, *If Democrats Had Any Brains*, 104.

distress). Then some of these Muslims do their damnedest to bring this all about.

- *Some* Jews believe that when the Messiah (the redeemer of Israel) comes, he must bring violence and war to their enemies, because, as the prophet Isaiah clearly states, the Day of Jubilee is also "the day of vengeance of our God" (Isa 61:2). Then some of these Jews do their damnedest to inflict their own mimetic vengeance for God's sake.

It is all either highly coincidental or, in fact, Girard's mimetic theory is correct in that enemies often resemble each other. In this case, it seems to be that sworn enemies model each other to a T.

Michael: I wholeheartedly agree with your assessment of things here. However, none of this means that experiencing an at-hand kingdom of God is *impossible*, even in the midst of suffering at the hands of others. The enlightened master *may even suggest* that true enlightenment is experiencing heaven in the midst of hell, in the midst of suffering of the greatest kind. Perhaps this is why, for example, Buddhist monk Thích Quang Duc could light himself on fire in protest of the persecution of Buddhists by the government of South Vietnam. Just listen to how David Halberstam powerfully describes the scene:

> I was to see that sight again, but once was enough. Flames were coming from a human being; his body was slowly withering and shriveling up, his head blackening and charring. In the air was the smell of burning human flesh; human beings burn surprisingly quickly. Behind me I could hear the sobbing of the Vietnamese who were now gathering. I was too shocked to cry, too confused to take notes or ask questions, too bewildered to even think ... As he burned he never moved a muscle, never uttered a sound, his outward composure in sharp contrast to the wailing people around him.[5]

---

5. Halberstam, *Making of a Quagmire*, 211.

Second Refrain

No matter whether the Buddhist monk is high atop a mountain, soaking in the divine all around him, or defying a corrupt government through self-immolation, it has been shown that he can get to such a place where heaven can be had no matter the circumstances.

Matthew: I recall hearing about this event some while back—powerful stuff. His testimony reminds me of Blandina's, an early Christian martyr:

> But the blessed Blandina, last of all, having, as a noble mother, encouraged her children and sent them before her victorious to the King, endured herself all their conflicts and hastened after them, glad and rejoicing in her departure as if called to a marriage supper, rather than cast to wild beasts. And, after the scourging, after the wild beasts, after the roasting seat, she was finally enclosed in a net, and thrown before a bull. And having been tossed about by the animal, on account of her hope and firm hold upon what had been entrusted to her, and her communion with Christ, she also was sacrificed. And the heathen themselves confessed that never among them had a woman endured so many and such terrible tortures.[6]

Michael: Like many Buddhists, it certainly seems that the early Christians were quite adept at experiencing the kingdom of heaven in spite of some horrific conditions.

Matthew: Indeed they were. And I think it is in large part because they held to the *belief* that they would be resurrected in the same way that Christ was. So death, not even death in the most torturous ways, could sway them or drive them out of the at-hand kingdom of God. Which brings me all the way back to my original point—belief matters. It *may* not be the primary thing we should

---

6. Pamphilius, *Church History*, 331.

Act II: Exploring Salvation

focus on, but it plays its part in all this. In fact, it can play a vital role in how we experience the universe right now.

Michael: Yes it does. Peace, my friend.

Matthew: And to you as well.

ACT III

Exploring Hell

Letter 11

The Authority of Scripture and Some Really Bad News

Michael,

As excited as I am to talk about hell—not!—I thought it best to first discuss a few other topics instead. Trust me—*says just about everyone right before they lie*—but really, I am not deflecting, for what I will be saying in this letter will be important in determining how we approach the fiery topic at hand. It would almost be criminal to simply open up to a place in our English Bible—such as Mark 9—read the word "hell," and call it a day. I know that is not what everyone does, and that there are great theologians who still affirm the doctrine of eternal torment, but because I also know many Christians who *do* employ this "hermeneutic"—if you can even call it that—this letter bears importance.

    The first thing worth mentioning is that the way in which one defines the "authority of Scripture" will matter when it comes to thinking about anything doctrinally, including hell. What scriptural authority means for many in the Protestant tradition is that the Bible is the inerrant and infallible Word of God. Here are but a few of the "Articles" from the *Chicago Statement on Biblical Inerrancy,* which state this very thing:

63

- Article I: We affirm that the Holy Scriptures are to be received as the authoritative Word of God.

- Article XI: We affirm that Scripture, having been given by divine inspiration, is infallible, so that, far from misleading us, it is true and reliable in all matters it addresses.

- Article XII: We affirm that Scripture in its entirety is inerrant, being free from all falsehood, fraud, or deceit.

- Article XIV: We affirm the unity and internal consistency of Scripture.[1]

Some Christians are a bit more "liberal," and refrain from going so far as to affirm everything in the *Chicago Statement*, but then still call the Bible the "word of God." Regardless, most Protestants seem to believe that if it is in the Bible, it is theologically 100 percent accurate, 100 percent of the time—*God said it, I believe it, and that settles it*. This includes all of the divinely mandated violence found in the book of Joshua; it includes God giving a covenant of peace to Phinehas after Phinehas murders an interracial couple in Numbers 25; and it includes the many instances—the flood of Noah and the firebombing of Sodom and Gomorrah, being two such stories—where entire populations of people are divinely executed for being corrupt and violent. These are just some of the "hard truths in the Bible," as I have often been told. *Huh?* I am sorry, but if we believe in an eternal God (Heb 13:8), then how could anyone suggest, on the one hand, that God did these horrifically violent things, but on the other hand is *fully* revealed by a nonviolent Christ Jesus (see John 5:19–20, 6:38, 8:28, 10:29, 12:49; Col 2:9)?

I just don't get it.

Anyway, to my point: because there is this Janus-faced view of God—where he has a violent, vengeful streak, as *the Bible clearly states*—eternal hell seems like a natural fit, does it not? At least, it seems like a plausible scenario. Additionally, we have not even mentioned how the book of Revelation gets interpreted by most

---

1. *The Chicago Statement on Biblical Inerrancy* can be found at http://www.reformed.org/documents/index.html?mainframe=http://www.reformed.org/documents/icbi.html.

Evangelicals, where the "God of the Old Testament" is coming back, with *guns blazing*. It seems everyone and their brother is getting the divine version of *The People's Elbow*,[2] thrown into a lake of fire, a place chock full of evil beasts and false prophets (Rev 19:17–21).

I do not just brush off all of these verses from the Hebrew Bible and the book of Revelation because I am some "typical liberal," *as I have often heard*. My cards have been placed on the table regarding both.[3] The point in mentioning all this is to simply and humbly concede, and say *yes, if you want to find biblical evidence for eternal hell, you can find it*. But that does not mean you will fail in finding evidence that some people are, in the end, simply *annihilated*. And neither of these details then changes the fact that the Bible also gives us evidence that *all people will one day be reconciled to God*. Indeed, there is scriptural evidence for all three positions—ECT, CI, and UR. Here's a handy-dandy table:[4]

Eternal Conscious Torment	Conditional Immortality	Universal Reconciliation
"Many of those who sleep in the dust of the earth shall awake, some to everlasting life, and some to shame and everlasting contempt." ~ Dan 12:2	"And these will go away into eternal punishment, but the righteous into eternal life." ~ Matt 25:46	"Who must remain in heaven until the time of universal restoration that God announced long ago through his holy prophets." ~ Acts 3:21

---

2. The people's elbow was the finishing move of wrestling legend, The Rock.

3. See *All Set Free*, pp 94–95, for one such instance.

4. In the documentary *Hellbound?*, filmmaker Kevin Miller compiles a list of Bible verses in favor of the three major Christian eschatological views, namely ECT, annihilationism (or Conditional Immortality, from henceforth labeled CI), and universal reconciliation. In favor of ECT, he lists Isaiah 66:24, Daniel 12:2, Matthew 5:22; 29–30; 7:13; 10:28; 13:38–42, 49–50; 25:31–46; Mark 9:43–45, and Luke 12:5; 16:19–26. For CI, he lists: Matthew 19:29–30; 25:46, John 3:16, 36; 4:14; 5:24; 6:40, 47, 54, 68; 10:28, and Romans 5:21. For UR, he lists: John 12:32, Acts 3:21, Romans 5:18; 11:32, 1 Corinthians 15:22–28, 2 Corinthians 5:19, Philippians 2:9–11, 1 Timothy 2:4, Titus 2:11, Hebrews 2:9, 1 John 2:2, and 1 Peter 3:9.

Act III: Exploring Hell

Eternal Conscious Torment	Conditional Immortality	Universal Reconciliation
"And these will go away into eternal punishment, but the righteous into eternal life." ~ Matt 25:46	"For God so loved the world that he gave his only Son, so that everyone who believes in him may not perish but may have eternal life." ~ John 3:16	"Who desires everyone to be saved and to come to the knowledge of the truth. For there is one God; there is also one mediator between God and humankind, Christ Jesus, himself human, who gave himself a ransom for all." ~ 1 Tim 2:4
"And if your foot causes you to stumble, cut it off; it is better for you to enter life lame than to have two feet and to be thrown into hell. And if your eye causes you to stumble, tear it out; it is better for you to enter the kingdom of God with one eye than to have two eyes and be thrown into hell, where their worm never dies, and the fire is never quenched." ~ Mark 9:45–48	"Very truly, I tell you, anyone who hears my word and believes him who sent me has eternal life, and does not come under judgment, but has passed from death to life." ~ John 5:24	"And I, when I am lifted up from the earth, will draw all people to myself." ~ John 12:32
"But I will warn you whom to fear: fear him who, after he has killed, has authority to cast into hell." ~ Luke 12:5	"I give them eternal life, and they will never perish. No one will snatch them out of my hand." ~ John 10:28	"And he is the atoning sacrifice for our sins, and not for ours only but also for the sins of the whole world." ~ 1 John 2:2

In light of this, I think a fair place to begin a conversation about hell is by admitting that it is not all that *clear* and perhaps, even, there is a biblical trajectory that is—gasp!—progressive. And that progression is away from a vengeful God and toward a God that is just like Jesus.

Perhaps.

AUTHORITY OF SCRIPTURE AND SOME REALLY BAD NEWS

Now, before turning it back over to you, I wanted to change gears a bit and make a second point about hell. It will be brief. What I do not understand is that in spite of the fact that there is *not much* emphasis placed on any notion of hell in Jewish thought,[5] somehow when the Gospel of Jesus is introduced, it all of a sudden plays a *vital role*, according to many Christians. You see, the "common" Jewish thought was that everyone went to *Sheol*.[6] It simply means "the grave" (In Greek, *Hades* is the equivalent). But, according to the vast majority of Christians, in comes the Gospel, and with it, this really *terrible* news—you will end up burning forever if you do not accept said gospel. But I thought Gospel literally meant "good news," and came from the Greek noun *euangelion*? Perhaps if there was an *already* developed doctrine of ECT, then the coming of Jesus, and thus, *potential* salvation, would be *euangelion,* but I cannot help but think it is an improper word if, at the advent of the Gospel, an eternal torture chamber came along with it. Yet, this seems to be the case according to most Christians.[7] I find that perplexing to say the least.

I think I have said what I needed to say before introducing the word that most English Bibles translate as "hell." But talking about Jesus' use of the word *Gehenna* will have to wait until my next letter, as it will take the entirety of the letter to fully do the word justice. What I would like to do now is turn it over to you. I am curious as to what your take on hell is. What is it? Where is it? Is it even a place, or rather, a state of being? Surely, you need not believe in such a place of torment, as you've stated before, but you

---

5. This is not to say that no Jew believed in an afterlife punishment. In fact, after the exile into Babylon, some Jews picked up some of the beliefs of the Babylonians, including a posthumous punishment-by-fire. This is depicted quite heavily in the non-biblical book of 1 Enoch. But this doctrine was in no way developed to the degree the doctrine of ECT is today.

6. See, for instance, Psalm 139:7–8, which reads: "Where can I go from your spirit? Or where can I flee from your presence? If I ascend to heaven, you are there; if I make my bed in Sheol, you are there."

7. In letter 15, I will address the doctrine of CI, as not all non-Universalists adhere to the doctrine of ECT.

Act III: Exploring Hell

must have *something* to say on the topic, even if it is as dissimilar to Western Christianity's view as the East is from the West.

"May the Lord give strength to his people!
May the Lord bless his people with peace!"
~ Psalm 29:11

Shalom, dear friend,

Matthew

Letter 12

Hell: Eternal Torture or Annoying Distraction?

Matthew,

I vacillate between four emotions when the subject of hell comes up: tickled, angered, excited, and annoyed. The first year or so of my Universalism was characterized by polar opposites, anger and excitement. On the one hand, I was thrilled by the possibility of a God who was perfectly loving and gracious, and could accomplish his desire to have everyone be saved and come to the knowledge of the truth (1 Tim 2:4). On the other hand, though, I was equally angered when people would attack and try to take away this possibility. With greater understanding and a growing circle of support, I eventually found the possibility of everlasting torture to be quite humorous, bordering on absurd. Let me correct myself, it is entirely absurd. At the present moment, I find the subject to be primarily an annoying distraction. Frankly, I am tired of thinking about the heavenly life in such a negative way, in what it is *not* like. And in a very practical way, I have discovered that obsession with such a subject is dangerous and an indication of sickness.

    Let me explain.

    There seems to be a natural law that people gravitate towards whatever they focus on. Perhaps this is what is known as the law of attraction and indeed, it seems true of both "mental" and "physical" activities. For example, when a driver is navigating a road, her primary focus should not be on the other cars and obstacles (hell), but on the open spaces where she wants her car to go (heaven). It might be said that taking some note of where the other drivers are is necessary to be safe, but really, as long as the open spaces fill the driver's consciousness, what the rest of the world is up to is not strictly relevant, and indeed a rather dangerous thing to focus on. *To focus on the obstacles of life is to guarantee a collision with them.*

Or, take my preoccupation with everything that can go wrong in life. I have seen marked improvement over the years, but much of my life has been an exercise in avoiding the embarrassment of failure, rather than attempting a positive good. And look at how my life has turned out. I have a stress-free but largely unfulfilling job and the list of things I would like to accomplish in this life has remained unchanged. It seems I have missed the obstacle of failure by careening into the obstacle of fear.

Nothing good comes from dwelling on a negative. People are not made better when they are forced to operate under fear. Your daughter, Elyse, is a shining example. She knows nothing of an eternal lake of fire and yet, it has never occurred to me that she might need a stronger parenting hand. She is still a child, of course, and sometimes acts childishly, but how can that be shown to be a grievous fault? Everyone has to "grow up," after all. Something deep within me knows that should she all of a sudden be taught that there is a burning lake of fire awaiting all the people who do not believe in Jesus, she would suffer great psychological and spiritual torment. I am certain that you agree with me, given your many childhood anecdotes regarding this very thing.

In addition, authentic and spontaneous living—the type of life so prized by people in the East and evident in children everywhere—is impossible under a rule of fear. Under fear, my motivation for everything that I do is simply to not get squashed like a bug, or zapped with a thunderbolt. It is not that I love God—or, Zeus, more like it—I am just afraid of what he can do to me. It is only since I have broken free of this trap that I've recognized fear itself to be hell. Or, at least, fear is underneath all the various ways in which we experience the many hells of this life.

Once again, Buddhism, in contrast, breathes a breath of sanity.

Ahhhh . . .

Buddhism, as I personally understand it, has no concept of divine judgment after death, unless you consider reincarnation to be a type of judgment—the worthy, enlightened souls escape the wheel of samsara, while the unenlightened remain chained. It borrows its cosmology from Hinduism, which says that life is essentially a drama, a game of God playing hide-and-go-seek with herself. G.K. Chesterton (a Christian) agrees, and puts it like this: "God has written, not so much a poem, but rather a play; a play he had planned as perfect, but which has necessarily been left to human actors and stage managers who have since made rather a mess of it."[1] This is a view of life that makes intuitive sense. If God is almighty and everlasting, then what has she got to do with her time but to entertain herself? And what better game than to totally lose herself, and then try to find her way back. It says that everyone is a part of the godhead, so everyone is participating in this heavenly game.

That being said, the sanity of a God who would basically be torturing a part of *herself*—in the way that many Christians view the final destruction of the ones made in her very *image*—would truly have to be questioned. In this respect, Buddhism and many forms of Christianity are not compatible. And, might I say, the choice between the two is frankly painless.

I have faith, however, that Buddhism and Christianity, as properly understood by folks such as yourself, only have *few* points of contention. So please, as you promised at the end of your previous letter, expound a concept of hell that would fit within a robust Christianity.

"Be steadfast, immovable, always excelling in the work of the

---

1. Chesterton, *Orthodoxy*, 78.

Act III: Exploring Hell

Lord, because you know that in the Lord your labor is not in vain."
~ 1 Corinthians 15:58

Blessings and Peace,

Michael

Letter 13

What in the Hell Is Hell?

Michael,

First off, please do not beat yourself up over "careening into the obstacle of fear." Remember, it is you who taught me that "the soul will grow at its own pace, thank you very much." And regardless, per my observations, you have since careened off of the obstacle of fear and into a pool of realization. You are, after all, in the midst of publishing your first book, and, call me biased, but I enjoy it very much.

That being said, it seems correct to say that hell, regardless of what that may metaphysically mean, is merely a distraction. To add my own analogy, believing in hell is like a when sports team plays to not lose, rather than playing to win. The other day, my beloved Tottenham Hotspur did this against Chelsea FC. They were up 2–0 at halftime and during the second half, began dropping their defense deeper and deeper into their own zone, playing completely defensive. Sure enough, Chelsea scored two goals in the second half and Tottenham had to settle for a draw. In the Spurs' attempt to "not lose," they lost the lead that was actually built by playing on the front foot, as they say. Hell, then, with its roots grounded in fear, is sort of like that.

Act III: Exploring Hell

But here is the crux of things: hell is real. *Really, it is!* Because the mind is so powerful, and because so many people hold to this doctrine like the sacred cow that it is, it becomes manifested in very real ways. Just think of how many people have been abused by of the doctrine of hell. "Heretics" have even been put to death with hell used as a justification. The great philosopher Thomas Aquinas argues for this very practice in *The Summa Theologica*:

> I answer that, with regards to heretics two points must be observed: one, on their own side; the other, on the side of the Church. On their own side there is the sin, whereby they deserve not only to be separated from the Church by excommunication, but also to be severed from the world by death. For it is a much graver matter to corrupt the faith which quickens the soul, than to forge money, which supports temporal life. Wherefore if forgers of money and other evil-doers are forthwith condemned to death by the secular authority, much more reason is there for heretics, as soon as they are convicted of heresy, to be not only excommunicated but even put to death.[1]

And so, because of this doctrine, hell has manifested as the burning of human beings on stakes in public squares. Sadly, that is very real. And might I mention, given Aquinas' logic, the death of Jesus even seems justified, for could we not say that:

> I answer that, with regards to [*this blasphemer*] two points must be observed: one, on his own side; the other, on the side of the [*Jewish*] faith. On his own side is the sin, whereby he deserves not only to be separated from his people by excommunication, but also to be separated from the world by death. For it is a much graver matter to corrupt the [*Jewish*] faith which quickens the soul, than to be a [*dissident of Rome*], which keeps [*Pax Romana*]. Wherefore if [*dissidents*] and other evil-doers are forthwith condemned to death by the secular authority, much more reason is there for [*blasphemers*], as soon as they

---

1. Aquinas, *Summa Theologica, Secunda Secundae Partis*, Question 11, Article 3.

are convicted of [*blasphemy*], to be not only excommunicated but even put to death [*on a cross*].

This should give us great pause.

So, while I share your annoyance in the very topic—and I do!—I feel as if I am one of those people who have been "called" to unteach this monstrous doctrine. I believe that you are as well.

Let us get to the unteaching then.

I recently posted the following on Facebook and I feel as if it fits as an introduction to what I want to say in this letter.

> Every person who has ever ended up in Gehenna, or the Valley of Hinnom as its known in Hebrew, has been put there by human beings. That should come into play when discussing this, no?[2]

As you know, the New Testament word translated to hell in our English Bibles is "Gehenna." Other than one instance where James uses it (Js 3:6), it is exclusive to Jesus. It is interesting to note that Paul never mentions it, nor does he offer the Gentiles a similar analogy that they could understand, yet also claims to "have fully proclaimed the gospel of Christ" (Rom 15:19, see also Acts 20:27). But, regardless, it is a term that indeed has a long and troubling history for Jews.

You see, on two separate occasions, the city of Jerusalem was utterly destroyed by foreign armies and the inhabitants were thrown into Gehenna. The first time was in the late sixth-century BCE (Babylon) while the second was in 70 CE (Rome), less than one generation after the death of Jesus. This is important because often, when Christians so flippantly use the word "hell," they pay no mind to this context. And this context is important because much of what Jesus had to say about "hell" was with the coming destruction of Jerusalem in mind. To not acknowledge that is to not acknowledge that Jesus was a true prophet, and prophets tend to quote previous prophets. With regards to this, my friend and scholar Brad Jersak points out how Jesus "cites or alludes to every

---

2. https://www.facebook.com/matthew.distefano.7/posts/852270978228549.

chapter in Jeremiah where Hinnom is mentioned."[3] And for Jeremiah, Hinnom was the subject of his very real admonitions. Sadly, because Jeremiah was dismissed by his interlocutors, his warnings would actually come to pass as Hinnom would become the place where the Babylonians burned the bodies of the Jews after Jerusalem fell. *Sound familiar?* It should, as this same thing happened after Jesus' interlocutors failed to heed Jesus' warnings. So hell in this sense is manmade. It can be called Gehenna or it can be called Auschwitz, Stalin's Gulags, or the killing fields of Cambodia. But it is essentially the same thing.

That being said, Jesus does also seem to engage the Jewish tradition that believed Gehenna represented afterlife punishment. This is known as the Enoch tradition. However, Jesus does not just let that tradition rest on its laurels, but actually subverts its teachings. (He had a tendency to do such things.) In Mark 9:49, after warning others about hell, Jesus *clearly states* that "everyone will be salted with fire." You read that right: *everyone*. This was not a part of the Enoch tradition![4] Not only does he say this, but then he qualifies it by saying that the salt produced from the fire is good (Mark 9:50). You read that right: *it is good*. And everyone who goes into the fire gets salted by it. Or, as Paul would later write in 1 Corinthians 3:12–15 (emphasis mine):

> Now if anyone builds on the foundation with gold, silver, precious stones, wood, hay, straw—the work of each builder will become visible, for the Day will disclose it, because it will be revealed with fire, and the fire will test what sort of work each has done. If what has been built on the foundation survives, the builder will receive a reward. If the work is burned up, the builder will suffer loss; *the builder will be saved, but only as through fire*.

So, again, everyone passes through the fire: for Paul, so that they may be saved from the wood, hay, and straw that ultimately amounts to nothing and for Jesus, so that they may be saved from a lack of salt, that is, from their own sin. In this sense, then, perhaps

3. Jersak, "Salted with Fire," para. 6.
4. See 1 Enoch 56:7–8; 63:10; 99:11.

the fire that we are thrown into is God's very presence. After all, God is described, on numerous occasions, as an eternal fire (Deut 4:24; Heb 12:29). And for some, I believe experiencing this would be tormenting, as sloughing the filth and grim off of a precious gem no doubt would be.[5] The writer of Hebrews puts it like this: "Now, discipline always seems painful rather than pleasant at the time, but later it yields the peaceful fruit of righteousness to those who have been trained by it" (Heb 12:11).

Much more could be said about this topic. But this is not really the project for such deep exegetical work. I will simply conclude by saying that I do believe those who find resonance in Buddhism and those who profess Christianity (as I understand the Christian faith) can find commonality on this subject. While there are differences—I believe there is a purification process that does occur after this life, while the Buddhist *may* not necessarily affirm this—I do not believe these differences stand in our way. Both have much to say about the here and now, which includes a here and now that can be hell. The Christian calls it Gehenna while perhaps the Buddhist would attribute it to vast negative Karma, or even Naraka (in some schools of Buddhist thought). But the enlightened from each faith tradition certainly have a lot to say about how to avoid such a fate.

Perhaps now we can focus our attention on the topic of justice and how that plays into this discussion. What I am curious about are your thoughts on how God can be called *just* in our eschatological model. In other words, doesn't justice demand hell? Or, is this a ridiculous notion?

May the flames of God burn forever,

Matthew

---

5. I will note that the word "torment" comes from the Greek word *básanos*, which originally was a touchstone used to test the purity of precious metals.

Letter 14

Musings about Justice

Matthew,

In many ways, the secular world is more in tune with the ways of God than the religious world. Questions like "How can a good/loving/just God send people to hell for eternity?" should give Christians much greater pause than they do.[1] But instead, they tend to write them off with the assumption that because God is so much superior than we are, no progress can be made toward understanding God's ways. After all, as the saying goes: "His ways are higher than our ways" (Isa 55:8–9). We need to make a distinction, however, between a God whose ways are higher and a God whose ways are merely different. If God's goodness was merely different from our goodness, God's love merely different from our love, God's justice merely different from our justice, what would be the point in striving for the perfection of these things and how would we know when we got there?

---

1. I realize that Arminians will contend that people send themselves to hell, so to speak. Ultimately though, no one who believes in such a place can avoid the fact that such a place/state exists to begin with. For even if people send themselves, the question is raised: "Why does God, who is love, conjure up such an existence?" And if God is the ultimate cause of everything—in a dual-causation universe of course—then he is still *ultimately* and perhaps even primarily responsible should people "send themselves to hell."

Musings about Justice

As I understand it though, and as C.S. Lewis points out in *The Problem of Pain*, the reality is that it is like we are all trying to draw a perfect circle, free-hand.[2] God is the perfect circle and no matter how close we get, we can never draw a precisely perfect one. With practice though, we become more and more proficient at goodness, love, and justice, and we know that we are getting better and better because, among other things, we have had it modeled for us by Jesus, who the Apostle Paul called "the fullness of God in bodily form" (Col 2:9). Perhaps our first attempts at justice, then, will not rise above retribution. But with time, practice, and a new vision, we make strides toward complete restoration, the justice of a higher, more divine, form.[3]

It is impossible to escape our humanity and the terms that we use to describe the world around us. So, if God has a different working definition of justice than we do, that is, if his justice is separate from his goodness, or if he values retribution over restoration, and we have no access to this—experiential or otherwise—then there is not much we can do about it. For example, how can a species, who recognizes that sociologically, restoration is a higher, more humane form of justice than retribution,[4] understand God if he completely begs to differ? The best we can say is that, as per our definition, God is acting unjustly. Perhaps he would say the same of us!

Either way, we would seem be at an impasse.

All of this is to say that according to our own human terminology, a God who would inflict infinite punishment for finite

---

2. Lewis, *Problem of Pain*, 30.

3. For a detailed look at the concept of divine justice, see the following essays from *Stricken by God?: Nonviolent Identification and the Victory of Christ*: "The Repetition of Reconciliation, Satisfying Justice, Mercy, and Forgiveness" by Sharon Baker, "Forgiveness, Reconciliation and Justice" by Miroslav Volf, and "Freed to Be Human and Restored to Family: The Saving Significance of the Cross in a Honduran Barrio" by Mark D. Baker.

4. Recent studies into various prison systems show this very thing. See Washington Post article "The Netherlands has a Strange Problem: Empty Prisons," published July 8, 2016, which can be found at https://www.washingtonpost.com/news/worldviews/wp/2016/07/08/the-netherlands-have-a-strange-problem-empty-prisons/?utm_term=.881bfeaa0a6d.

crimes is unjust. The secular world understands that the scales of justice are imbalanced—even if we are thinking in purely retributive terms. Remember, perfect retribution is literally "an eye for an eye," or as close to that as possible.[5] Hence, even a retributively "just" God would limit the punishment to the degree of the crime and since the crimes are not infinite, the punishment should not be either.

That being said, people indeed ought to know when they are in the wrong. *Absolutely!* That is a requirement for justice. But punishment in and of itself does *nothing* to bring about this knowledge. What is needed is clarity (which can be a form of "punishment" itself), and ultimately, mercy. Or, as Scottish theologian George MacDonald puts it, "God does punish sin, but there is no opposition between punishment and forgiveness. The one may be essential to the possibility of the other."[6]

Let me be clear: forgoing retributive punishment, assuming there is appropriate remorse, does not mean that the criminal gets away with anything. Remorse is really the only thing that can act as a "payment" anyway. I admit, this is not a comfortable model of justice to always live with. It states that the sinner indeed has to live with his wrongdoing and the victim has to live with being wronged—as well as living with the victimizer who did the wrongdoing. This is not easy! But, as biblical scholar Sharon Baker points out in *Executing God*, it is indeed a higher and deeper form of justice than retribution: "Whereas retributive justice seeks to fit the punishment to the crime, attempting to control wrongdoing through punishment, restorative justice forgives the crime

---

5. As philosopher Thomas Talbott points out: "Contrary to popular belief, the Old Testament principle of retaliatory justice—'an eye for an eye and a tooth for a tooth'—was never instituted for the purpose of justifying harsh punishment for serious crimes, something that no one at the time would have questioned; instead, it was instituted for the purpose of eliminating excessive punishment, such as capital punishment in exchange for a tooth. The idea was very simple. We must measure the seriousness of a crime according to the degree of harm done, and we must proportion the punishment to the seriousness of the crime." (Talbott, *Inescapable Love of God*, 138)

6. MacDonald, *Unspoken Sermons*, 248.

and seeks to redeem wrongdoing through a repairing of the relationship."[7] This is what the Bible has taught me. It is what Jesus modeled. So, as the prophet Isaiah says, God's ways *are* higher than our ways (Isa 55:9), thus, his justice should always be thought of in the highest of ways—not merely different or, dare I suggest, lower, but higher, and deeper, and wider. In other words, God's justice is *restorative*.

I hope that answers the questions you posed at the end of your previous letter. Perhaps this collection can conclude with an expansion on the thoughts presented here. What are your views regarding justice, and how does this view help lead you to the conclusions you hold? I look forward to what you have to say.

"May justice roll down like waters, and righteousness like an ever-flowing stream."

~ Amos 5:24

Until next time,

Michael

---

7. Baker, *Executing God*, 93–94.

Letter 15

Justice, Freedom, and the Implications for Humankind

Michael,

I agree with you that God's version of justice, being higher than humankind's, is for the purpose of restoration. I believe that is Paul's vision in Romans 11:34, when he describes God's compassionate judgments as "unsearchable"—no doubt unsearchable *because* of God's desire for mercy (Rom 11:32), as opposed to the manmade desire for vengeance (Heb 12:24).

    That being said, there is still something we need to address in this collection, which is the doctrine that states God is good, his justice seemingly restorative, yet in spite of this, that some people ultimately choose to continue in their wretched state and thus will just fade out of existence entirely. In essence, they will be annihilated, not by God's doing, but by their own "free" will that leads them down a path ending in destruction—*in the most literal sense.*

    As I understand things, this view seems to hinge on an understanding of free will that simply is not reality. Sure, it appears—on the surface at least—that the choices we make are derived from a will that is autonomous, our own and only our own. That is to say, we are in control of our will. But once we dig deeper into the interconnected human mind, this post-Kantian understanding is exposed as a façade. (I believe we covered this enough in Act 1, so I'll not add more here.)

Furthermore, this sort of libertarian free will that many believe we have does not seem to mesh all too well with what is taught in the Bible. It is not that the Scriptures fail in discussing the will in relation to freedom. Far from it. It is just that what they teach is humankind experienced a "fall"—or, to use C.S. Lewis' language, became "bent"[1]—and we are all enslaved, in one way or another, to sin. I like Paul's use of the phrase "powers and principalities" in best explaining what holds us captive (Eph 6:12). This raises the question: "If we are enslaved, how can our will be 'free?'" Well, that is where the Gospel comes in. It is about being *set free from something*, and that true freedom is found, not in the simple ability to do "good" or "evil," but in doing as God does, as modeled by Christ Jesus. Drawing from Tolkien, professor of English Literature, Donald T. Williams, makes the following observation:

> The essence of human freedom within the powers of the world . . . is illustrated in Frodo's struggle on Amon Hen. His will seems overpowered both by the call of the Eye of Sauron wanting to find him and a voice commanding him to take off the ring so that Sauron will fail to do so. "The two powers strove in him. For a moment, perfectly balanced between their piercing points, he writhed, tormented. Suddenly he was aware of himself again. Frodo, neither the Voice nor the Eye: free to choose and with one remaining instant in which to do so. He took the Ring off his finger."[2] We find the essence of our humanity, our identity as children of Iluvatar, in those moments when, neither voice nor eye, we show our freedom within the bounds of the world by choosing the right.[3]

If free will were about simply having the ability to choose good or evil, right or wrong, peace or violence, love or fear, etc., then sure, perhaps one could "freely" become so wicked that they essentially

---

1. Lewis, *Out of the Silent Planet*, 140.
2. Tolkien, *Fellowship of the Ring*, 472.
3. Williams, *Mere Humanity*, 124–25.

Act III: Exploring Hell

lose their humanity and perish entirely. But if freedom is found in having the ability to say yes to God and the things of God, we must think someone with free will in this sense would always choose God. To put it this way, if Gollum could truly ever see things the way they were before discovering the Ring, he no doubt would choose to go back to before he slew Deagol, to before he was corrupted and enslaved. And if God is *just*, then I must also think that he will afford everyone, including Smeagol, the freedom in the end to make such a choice.

Yet, in the annihilationism model, there seems to be little said about restorative justice at all—and I find this to be a problem. It does not appear that the wicked are brought to a point of contrition for their sins, which, as you stated, is the very point of restorative justice in the first place. That is, unless they do so and *then* become annihilated, but that does not seem just either. For if the wicked—those like Charles Manson, Adolf Hitler, and Saul of Tarsus—are evil for snuffing out life, how is God good if he, either actively or passively, responds in kind?

In addition, it also does not appear that those in "heaven" ever have to deal with any potential mess they themselves may have created for the ones annihilated. How, then, could a just God allow some humans to experience union with him, while at the same time—because of our interconnectedness—be partially responsible for others being annihilated? Are we not our brother's keeper (Gen 4:9)? Where is the justice in that? It would appear the just thing would be for those "lost" to be able to make a choice about God *void* of the destructive harm caused by those "saved," and also for the "saved" to have to reconcile with the ones they've harmed (the lost). That is how the heavenly life is achieved in the here and now, so I hope it is the same after we pass, lest we find "the afterlife" to in fact be rather hellish, seemingly lacking justice altogether. Christian missionary Sadhu Sundar Singh seems to agree, and then puts forth a beautiful exposé as to how the damned will, instead than being annihilated out of existence, in the end freely choose the good, or in other words, God:

However bad and evil-living a man may be, there is in man's nature a divine spark or element which is never inclined toward sin. His conscience and spiritual feelings may become dulled and dead, but this spark of the divine is never extinguished. This is why even in depraved criminals there is always some good to be found. It has been noticed that some of those who have committed murders with the utmost violence and savagery have often generously aided the poor and oppressed. If this divine spark or element cannot be destroyed, then we can never be hopeless for any sinner. If we say that it can be destroyed, then sorry at separation from God because of sin and the remorse of hell will never be felt, because for feeling this pain of sorry and remorse there is nothing in man but this spark—and hell will not be hell without this feeling. And, if he feels the pain, then, being tortured by it, sooner or later it will assuredly compel him to come to God for restoration.[4]

While I am eager to depart from this little distraction we call hell, could we first discuss the spiritual and psychological anguish ECT inflicts on those who adhere to such a view? I ask this because it was personally such a debilitating doctrine to hold to, so I feel I would be remiss not to mention a few of my most troubling anecdotes. Perhaps you feel the same. After that, we can move on to chatting about a more cheerful topic, namely, what this Reality is all about, and how we go about discovering God and the truths about God and the universe.

"May the grace of the Lord Jesus be with you. My love be with you in Christ Jesus."

~ 1 CORINTHIANS 16:23–24

Yours in Christ,

Matthew

4. Singh, *Meditations*, 57.

Third Refrain
The Torment of Eternal Torment

"Hell is pretty depressing. If you want to be happy, eh, just forgeddabout it."[1]

~ Jonathan Pearce

Michael: Regarding my prior belief in hell, I do not have any specific negative incidents to recount, but rather, a summation of twenty-five years. Speaking strictly from personal experience, the doctrine of ECT is excellent at one thing and one thing only, as a tool for taking the fun out of existence, and replacing it with fear. This is the worst thing imaginable. In *Universal Salvation? The Current Debate*, philosopher Thomas Talbott aptly labels it "objective horror."[2] Go ahead, put your hand over our Thursday night bonfire for just a moment and then meditate on how painful it would be to shove it all the way in. Most Western Christians will then tell you hell is worse than that—far worse! Meditate on the prospect of no relief from that pain. Ever. Not in a billion years,

---

1. Pearce, "Psychology of Religion," para. 13.
2. Talbott, *Universal Salvation?*, 5.

nor a trillion, nor any other absurdly large number you can think of. After all, you cannot count to infinity.

Now, if you are a sane person, you will do everything in your power to escape such a horrific fate. And so, your life will essentially be boiled down to nothing but a to-do list—go to church, share the "gospel," read the Bible, pray before bed, fast when inclined, perhaps get around to feeding the hungry, and worry that you have not forgotten anything. Or else! Furthermore, you also make sure you stick to the laundry-list of prohibitions—no smoking (especially pot), no swearing, no dancing, no R-rated movies, and no secular music. In a word, you strive to make life sanitary, lest you find yourself "backsliding."

Many of my experiences with Christianity seemed centered on hell avoidance.

But, once you escape this trap of fear, of hell, you can earnestly begin to question both lists. Aside from feeding the hungry, what is the concrete good of doing anything on the first list? What is the concrete evil of anything on the second? What if the behaviors on the second list were okay in moderation—or even outright indulgence from time to time—and what if during my Christian years I had been missing out on things that were never meant to be prohibited? What if life was meant to be a little dirty? And what if, heaven forbid, preaching the Gospel gets one a little dirty?

This makes me think that another way to interpret hell is that it is simply an absence of the fullness of life, here and now. Or, if you like, hell is what existence becomes when it is no longer fun, no longer joyous. And if that is indeed really how things are supposed to be, as so many Christians claim it is, I am not quite sure what the point of this life is. I thought this cosmos was ours to explore and cultivate, living as freely and fully as we can (Gen 1:28–30)?

Matthew: I believe you make a great point with regards to Western Christianity, in that it has become a giant list of dos and don'ts—which, mind you, is to miss the point of Jesus entirely. Sure, if you live with the freedom that God is love and that all will be well, you will probably be more likely to share the Gospel, feed the hungry, and so on, but you will not be doing these things because they are on your "to-do" list. Or that you need to do them in order to spare yourself from the flames of hell. Rather, you will do them because they naturally follow from living a well-regulated life aimed toward the one true God of the cosmos.

I am curious about two things. First, you mentioned how twenty-five years of your life was spent adhering to the doctrine of ECT, so my question is, when did this change? And what happened in your life that brought you out of this doctrine and into a vastly more inclusive understanding of Christianity? And second, I am curious to find out where your dad Ric—a Christian Universalist author and philosopher—fits into your transformation story, if at all.

Michael: Rob Bell's *Love Wins* was responsible for my final "conversion," but my heart had been preparing for Universalism long before. In my final years before letting go of ECT, I remember listening to a Christian podcast in which the host thanked God for reminding us that the Christian life requires *effort*, and that studying the "word" was vitally important. It may be true within a certain context—as in, if one desires to be a biblical scholar—but at that moment, instead of encouraging me to "go deeper," it only made me weary. It was all too much. The yoke was too heavy—the praying, the fasting, the Bible studies, and on and on—and all I wanted to do was take a really long nap. So, to answer your question, it was in fact laziness that was a considerable factor in leading me to the Promised Land.

Neat, right?

Probing deeper, I asked myself how the church could have the nerve to peddle this lifestyle onto the world, and why we thought our way of life was worth saving people for. It seemed farfetched that in the presence of God's glory, we would still need to do so many works like fasting and reading the Bible and joining Bible studies—that so much effort would be *required*—so I did not understand why it was such a vital detail now. I was under

Third Refrain

the impression heaven was at-hand. Perhaps there is a time and place for everything, and maybe doing these spiritual disciplines gets you to a place where you realize you do not need them. But all in all, I remain a confused agnostic on why these works were so vital to a faith tradition whose theological lynchpin is *sola gratia*, or grace alone. Seems rather contradictory, does it not?

Now, to where my dad fits in to all this.

Well, I am happy to say that I had, and still have, his utmost support. This was especially true—or perhaps just more welcomed—during my most uncertain days. I respect his opinion so much so that the entire world could be against me and I would still be confident. Yet, even *if* my dad were not a Universalist, I would still hold my ground on this beautifully liberating doctrine. Such is the strength of the Universalist argument. But, thankfully my dad's philosophy and theology fit within my doctrinal beliefs; hence there is no conflict to have to deal with.

Matthew: What a blessing it is to have such resource at your disposal! That said, before I contribute my thoughts regarding the torment of eternal torment, I wanted to comment on the spiritual disciplines you mentioned above. The way I understanding such practices as fasting, praying, or even chanting the Psalms like the Franciscans do, is that, as you said, they are tools we use in order to get to a place where we really do not need them anymore. None of us, so far as I am aware, can simply become enlightened the moment we desire it. No one can live perfectly in what Richard Rohr would call the "naked now" without honing their mind and sharpening their awareness. So, perhaps early on in our journey, it takes some intentional meditation or chanting or praying or fasting to get us in the right space to "hear" God, but once we learn how to be present with God in all places of life, we can shed some of these practices. Or, then again, perhaps we will keep some simply because we enjoy them, and even need reminders from time to time.

It's something for us to chew on.

Now, with that, please allow me to get to the meat of what I have to say.

Act III: Exploring Hell

First off, there is a very valid reason as to why I have historically had such harsh things to say about ECT. In short, it is because this doctrine forced my youth to be shrouded in *torment* and *horror*. For instance, when I was just a wee lad, I suffered through horrible night terrors that to this day have my mom convinced I was demon-possessed. Then on top of that, there were your "traditional nightmares" that occurred at least once a week. And I do not know if you have ever experienced sleep paralysis, but if you have not, please consider yourself lucky. You literally feel as if a demon is sitting on your chest—if you have a worldview that states demons "exist," that is. And I did. Thank God that is no longer the case.

Interestingly, now that I do not believe in hell as ECT, or demons as ontological beings for that matter, those terrors that used to haunt me have gone the way of the dodo. I cannot call this a coincidence, and has even been quite the teacher! You see, doctrines should be healing in nature, not tormenting. They should be balms for our wounds, not salt and sandpaper. Both of the English words "doctor" and "doctrine" find their root in the Latin *doctrina*. If you were not aware, the primary thing for a doctor to always bear in mind is "Do no harm" (*primum non nocere*). Hell, then, certainly fails this aptitude test in the worst of ways. It did for me, at least, and since I cannot escape my own subjective experience—in fact, none of us can—how can I think otherwise? So, to quote Sweet Brown of YouTube fame, with regards to ECT: "Ain't nobody got time for that!"[3]

That being said, it is totally understandable why people hold fast to this terrifying doctrine. Fear can be a real *son-of-a-bitch*. Or, to put it much more eloquently, you once wrote, "The fear that correct belief is the ticket to Heaven is a powerful trap. The fear that 'you must believe in an everlasting hell in order to be saved' is the most powerful trap of all."[4]

And my friend, you are absolutely correct—*and people are trapped!*

3. https://www.youtube.com/watch?v=8cT_Ulmcrys.
4. Machuga, "Foreword," ix.

Third Refrain

Look closely enough and you will see the whites of people's theological knuckles as they tremblingly clinch this doctrine in their hands. See how people emotionally respond to our Universalism. More often than not, it will angrily be met with the incorrect accusation *to take away hell is to take away the Gospel*. In the more extreme cases, we are met with charges of *false teacher, wolf in sheep's clothing, child of satan, one with the devil, circle-jerking cultist*, and my personal favorite, "professor of word vomit, who, in all reality, is getting ninety percent of his info from Wikipedia or a bitter Rabbi who has no reason to revere Scripture as holy." I'm sorry, but that one made me laugh. What a fear-based trap people are living in! The evidence is obvious.

I *would* be willing to bet, though, that there are actually many of these same folks who *would internally like to* denounce ECT, but cannot bring themselves to earnestly and honestly address it. Although many, as atheist neuroscientist Sam Harris once pointed out, seem apathetic to the fact that the multitudes of their human family are going to burn in hell forever;[5] in their heart of hearts, it is probably not so cut and dried. Perhaps I am wrong, but I do not see how the thought of our sons and daughters, mothers and fathers, brothers and sisters, aunts and uncles, cousins, friends, and colleagues burning in hell fails in eliciting some visceral response that yells "No!" I just think Christians hide this subconscious response really well, out of fear that their doctrinal house of cards might come tumbling down, or that they themselves may end up burning in a place for daring to question its very existence.

How tormenting! And again, what a trap!

But *take comfort*, I want to tell these folks, for Jesus told us to "fear not." After all, with love, we have nothing to fear. In fact, perfect love casts our fear (1 John 4:18) and God is love (1 John 4:8).

So what the hell, hell!

For the sake of our sanity, then, let's see to it that the doctrine of ECT—that is to say, the doctrine of pure fear—soon becomes a thing of the past. I mean, are we not sick of beliefs like the

---

5. https://www.youtube.com/watch?v=yqaHXKLRKzg#t=92m5s.

Act III: Exploring Hell

following, from Jonathan Edwards' infamous sermon "Sinners in the Hands of an Angry God?"

> The God that holds you over the pit of hell, much as one holds a spider or some loathsome insect over the fire, abhors you, and is dreadfully provoked. His wrath towards you burns like fire, he looks upon you as worth of nothing else but to be cast into the fire. He is of purer eyes than to bear you in his sight; you are ten thousand times as abominable in his eyes as the most hateful, venomous serpent is in ours.
>
> You have offended him infinitely more than ever a stubborn rebel did his prince, and yet it is nothing but his hand that holds you from falling into the fire every moment. It is to be ascribed to nothing else that you did not go to hell the last night; that you were suffered to awake again in this world, after you closed your eyes to sleep. And there is no other reason to be given why you have not dropped into hell since you arose in the morning, but that God's hand has held you up. There is no other reason to be given why you have not gone to hell since you have sat here in the house of God provoking his pure eye by your sinful, wicked manner of attending his solemn worship. Yea, there is nothing else that is to be given as a reason why you do not this very moment drop down into hell.[6]

Crap like this has done enough damage, has ruined enough lives, and therefore should probably be included in the "wood, hay, and stubble" that needs to be burned out of existence (1 Cor 3:12). The one true God of the cosmos, the God who is wholly good, wholly merciful, wholly gracious, loving, compassionate, and whose loving-kindness endures forever (Ps 136:1), has been blasphemed enough.

Michael: If we could witness a shift away from ECT, that would be just dandy. And is the church not due for one? Was it not you who taught me that roughly every 500 years, Christianity goes through

---

6. Edwards, *The Works*, 458.

a major "reformation?" And per my calculations, we are getting close, are we not?

Matthew: Yes. In fact, the 500 year anniversary of Luther's "Ninety-five Theses" is coming up shortly, on Halloween, 2017 to be exact. Perhaps eliminating the Molechian notion of an eternal hellacious afterlife will be a major part of whatever this new reformation is or will be. At least, that is my hope. Grace and peace, my dear friend.

Michael: Likewise.

ACT IV

Exploring Reality

Letter 16

The "Meaning" of Life

Matthew,

I would like to begin this letter with a quote from Alan Watts, as I believe it epitomizes where I stand on the supposed "meaning of life," which needless to say is what we'll be exploring in this letter. He writes:

> The meaning of life is just to be alive. It is so plain and so obvious and so simple. And yet, everybody rushes around in a great panic as if it were necessary to achieve something beyond themselves. The funny thing is, they are not quite sure what they need to achieve, but they are devilishly intent on achieving it.[1]

So, first of all, I believe that there is no overarching meaning to life. Life is a concrete foundation and does not point to something else. In other words, you do not use life like a tool to get at something greater. This does not in any way diminish the value of life. Quite the contrary, in fact, as per my mind, it makes the entire situation much more breathtaking. It means that life is there to make of it what you want. You are not forced or coerced to do anything. Just dance the dance.

That said, there *are* three things my logical mind needs in order to view life in this way (the logical mind being where the ego likes to hang out). First, I take for granted that God is infinite and everlasting,

---

1. Watts, *Culture of Counter-culture*, i.

perfectly loving, and, in a non-Calvinistic way, all-powerful. Second, I hold fast that every human soul is eternal. And third, that God will work with and through me to bring about a fully restored *telos*, or end goal. Ultimately, I have to take all this on trust—as I cannot deductively prove these premises—but I think there is enough scriptural and experiential evidence to make them a reasonable starting place. Furthermore, if I did not start here, I am not sure I would be able to fully embrace the here and now, or in other words, the kingdom of heaven. If God was not perfect love, for example, the here and now would simply be a place I'd rather not spend time in, given that everything was *potentially* being run by a tyrant. If my soul has the potential to one day be snuffed out, then anxiety over my future demise would simply loom too large to handle.[2] And if we are not all headed toward eschatological shalom, then our "ending" would seem hopeless, and to be without hope is to indeed taste hell. To escape the "flames," then, I need all of these premises.

When I think about life with these assumptions in place, I realize that it does not make sense to be anxious about anything. It certainly makes no sense to take life somberly. God has nothing but time on his hands and because nothing can challenge his sovereignty, life becomes a dance, or a rhythm, or in Greek, *perichoresis*. This dance, then, is the meaning of life and to again quote Watts, "the whole point of dancing is the dance."[3] And in the midst of this dance, there remains no room for being anxious and somber. (Contrast this with what my former self believed, where life was a war, a high stakes game of the greatest kind, the results of course being severe anxiety and somberness.)

I have since discovered that eternality is *essential* for a regulated life. If your soul exists for only a short period of time, one of two things seems to happen, depending on your personality type. You either run around like a beheaded chicken, trying to suck in every experience you can without taking the time to actually enjoy it, or you

---

2. For a detailed look at what our anxiety over death does to the human mind, see Ernest Becker's *The Denial of Death* or Richard Beck's *The Slavery of Death*.

3. This quote can be found at https://www.youtube.com/watch?v=qHnIJe E3LAI.

The "Meaning" of Life

give up, not attempting anything. Just notice the folks who hold fast and tight to doctrines like eternal torment, where souls are cast off like filthy rags, to burn for all eternity. Many not only constantly seem busy with tasks menial in nature, their lives full of what Ernest Becker would call "frenetic, ready-made activity,"[4] but then generally seem apathetic about traversing to the depths of themselves, to the dirtiest and realest of places—perhaps for fear of what they might find.

Indeed, as we've discussed, fear is a most paralyzing trap.

On the contrary, when you discover that the infinite is yours to play around with, for as long as you want, you are finally able to relax and enjoy life, seeing that its value is self-evident. You do not have to be a glutton. You do not have to have that second or third or fourth beer out of fear that you may not experience beer again. You have time to really "feel" and get into the rhythms of life: *sleep* and *wakefulness*, *summer* and *winter*, *happiness* and *sorrow*, and yes, *life* and *death*.

So, in the end, when you have the peace that surpasses all understanding (Phil 4:7), all that is left to do is to experience life. It is a simple but difficult proposition, and its solution is found in the practice of meditation and mindfulness. Recent events in your life have given you some insight into both of these practices, if I am not mistaken, so maybe you could talk more about this.

"The Lord dwells in the hearts of all creatures and whirls them round upon the wheel of maya. Run to him for refuge with all your strength, and peace profound will be yours through his grace."[5]

~ Krishna

Grace and peace, my friend,

Michael

4. Becker, *Denial of Death*, 23.
5. Easwaran, *Bhagavad Gita*, 263.

Letter 17

Our Theology is not God, but it can Certainly Point in Her Direction

Michael,

From June 19–26, 2016, I attended another one of Michael Hardin's *Making Peace Conferences*, and without getting into the particulars, I will briefly say that it was, yet again, life altering. For the second year in a row, not only did I witness the healing effects of true "Christian" community being lived out with others, but I was also able to tap into knowledge from deep within myself to make some important theological and phenomenological connections that needed to be made.[1] And the beauty of this knowledge is that because it is something that God herself has placed in every single one of us, it is about as anti-Gnostic as it gets. Sure, it is special knowledge, but not special because only certain people have access to it. Rather, to put it in Johannine terms, it is knowledge we have because we are all "in Christ," and that Christ is in all of us.

As you just pointed out, to experience such a beautiful reality, however, requires mindfulness and meditation, a journeying *inward* into the temple of the soul. Because of this, only those who

---

1. I spoke about my experiences from the 2015 conference in an article entitled "The Power of Positive Mimesis" that can be found at https://www.ravenfoundation.org/the-power-of-positive-mimesis/.

Our Theology is not God

have practiced it can know what I am talking about, for, as Michael Polanyi taught, we indeed "know more than we can tell."[2]

What excites me the most about what I experientially discovered during the conference is this: *God is not so much "out there," but "in here."* God is not experienced as a *deus ex machina*, or in other words, as a god who comes down to us on a machine, only to depart when his tasks are done, but as the fire that dwells in each and every one of us. Eckhart Tolle reminds us that God is known, "not as something outside you but as your innermost essence."[3] Indeed, God is with us—*Emmanuel!*—even in our suffering and darkest places. The writer of John's Gospel puts it like this:

> In the beginning was the Word, and the Word was with God, and the Word was God. He was in the beginning with God. *All things* came into being through him, and without him not one thing came into being. What has come into being in him was life, and the life was the light of *all people*. The light shines in the darkness, and the darkness did not overcome it (emphasis mine).

Let's unpack this a bit.

First off, notice how this is a "rewrite" of Genesis 1:1, where "in the beginning" God created something. *Now* though, in the beginning was already a something, the Word. And this Word, or *Logos*, more accurately, has a context. For the Greek philosopher, the Logos was the structuring principle of reality, and it was to be thought of as violence.[4] For the Jew, the Logos could be interpreted as Torah, the written (and/or oral) law of God.[5] But in light of Jesus, the Logos is now known to be the Christ, and is the "life and light of all people."

All people.
Every. Single. One.
And what is this Logos all about, then?

---

2. Polanyi, *Tacit Dimension*, 4.
3. Tolle, *Power of Now*, 165.
4. Heraclitus, fragments DK22B53 and DK22B80.
5. See Hardin, *Jesus Driven Life*, 267–69.

Act IV: Exploring Reality

In short, it is the antithesis of violence, namely, peace and love. In spite of the apt Heraclitean assessment—that humanity structures our world on violence and that "war is the father and king of all"[6]—the true Christ, which is the "light of all people" (John 1:4), is nonviolent. And any war this Cosmic Christ fights is fought in the same manner lambs fight wars, that is, they don't. As Girard first noticed:

> The Johannine Logos is foreign to any kind of violence; it is therefore forever expelled, an absent Logos that never has had any direct, determining influence over human cultures. These cultures are based on the Heraclitean Logos, the Logos of expulsion, the Logos of violence, which, if it is not recognized, can provide the foundation of a culture. The Johannine Logos discloses the truth of violence by having itself expelled.[7]

When we go within ourselves, then, to where God through the Christ has chosen to reside, we will recognize our true nature as loving, joyous, peaceful, forbearing, kind, good, faithful, gentle, and in control. St. Paul called these the fruits of the Spirit (Gal 5:22–23), the writer of John's Gospel called this "the Way," and it is by these fruits that we can know whether we are living "in the Spirit" or not, whether we are following the Way, or not. The Spirit will always produce this type of fruit, never anything contrary or contradictory.

It is breathtaking when you meditate on this. And that is why we are correct in emphasizing meditation and mindfulness, for without these, passages like John 1:1–5 would become mere words. And these words, as profound as they may be, can only point at the Truth. But, like all language, this is ultimately a feeble attempt.

I'll turn this back over to you now. I am curious as to how you approach the practice of meditation—what are we are supposed to get from it? What have you gotten from it? Questions like these. As always, I look forward to what you have to say.

---

6. Heraclitus, fragment 53.
7. Girard, *Things Hidden*, 271.

"May the God of peace himself sanctify you entirely; and may your spirit and soul and body be kept sound and blameless at the coming of our Lord Jesus Christ."

~ 1 Thessalonians 5:23

Peace, love, and blessings,

Matthew

Letter 18

Meditation and Mindfulness

My dearest Matthew,

Not all questions deserve answers. Someone once told me that simply putting a noun, a verb, and a question mark next to each other does not necessarily make for a good question. "What *should* I do with my life?" would be one such example. At first, it seems like a first-class, responsible inquiry, but it reveals an assumption about the "meaning" of life that I find erroneous. It assumes that something *ought* to be done in life, that the present moment is not fully complete. As we discussed, I suppose the opposite to be true, and that the only "requirement" in life (if one wants to even call it that), is to pursue joyous love. To that end, since nothing really needs to be *done* in life, nothing necessarily needs to be *got* from meditation. Instead, the meditative experience will give you the space to experience whatever it is you are going to experience. How you then interpret this experience will depend on a few things—your awareness, your mindfulness, and so forth. Whatever knowledge that is gained is entirely tacit, or in other words, experiential. It is yours and yours alone. And so, the point of meditation is nothing more than a part of our fully engaging and *experiencing* life.

So again, I cannot say what you should be "getting" from meditation.

Meditation and Mindfulness

In the words of Nike, *just do it*.

At this point in my spiritual development, however, it *is* hard for me to see the sufficiency in every present moment, including the purposefully meditative ones. I think it would be *especially* difficult for, let's say, the relatively wealthy—people who have the means and access to all manners of entertainment. For them, it takes longer to realize that one cannot always be high on life, and that the substance of life is actually found in the more sober pursuits: of knowledge, of peace, of stillness, of centering and grounding, etc. But life can be so damn distracting, and it is difficult to find stillness in the midst of such constant noise.

And yet, in spite of this, I *have* learned that, as much as I love losing myself in exciting activities such as dirt biking, it *is* unrealistic to expect that sensation in all of life. And not only is it unrealistic, it actually sounds rather empty, because even as a novice meditator, still struggling with nowness, the merits of pursuing meditative stillness are obvious. I dare not miss this. Some perspective, as well as a grateful heart, is all that is needed. For example, I am grateful that my nights are spent in "boredom," at home in a meditative state, rather than on the "exciting" beaches of Normandy, or something to that effect.

Again, perspective.

Perhaps that is one answer to the question of evil. Perhaps we live this life of death and sorrow in order to cultivate a grateful heart. When we taste and see how bad things *could* be, the present moment is transformed from drudgery to joy. Furthermore, hope for a "better time" keeps us, like the members of *The Fellowship of the Ring*, moving forward. And perhaps, even, only one life on this fallen earth is enough to cause eternal gratitude.

I remain tentative, however, because I would not want to state that this present, "boring" moment indeed requires a previous, "bad" moment to be livable. After all, is heaven not always at hand? And if so, then it would seem that we do not need relativity to be content.

That is to say, good does not require evil, so evil must remain an absurdity.

Act IV: Exploring Reality

Direct experience is the only thing needed to know this. When you meditate, for example, all the noise of the world gets drowned out, exposing the naked now to be concept free. Abstractions get overpowered by what can only be described as love, or if you like, God. Evil, then, being an abstraction, is always and only born from a concept, not reality, and is found to be an absurdity that has no place in the perpetually at-hand kingdom of heaven. In fact, being a privation rather than a reality, it is the very antithesis of it. But like darkness, once the light of heaven shines through, evil vanishes. To use biblical language, one could say that Satan falls like lightning (Luke 10:18).

The spiritually mature know this. No doubt, they have learned through reveling in the most boring thing of all: sitting and breathing. That is where the practice of meditation begins. Sit upright, balancing your torso on your buttocks. Keep your vision trained a couple of inches in front of you. Breathe in and out, noticing the sensation of each inhalation and exhalation. If a thought enters your mind, that is okay. Recognize it but do not hold onto it. Bring the mind back to the breath, and do not reprimand yourself. That is only the ego holding on.

You may then want to write about your experience, again, without condemnation or invasive questioning. Just write, letting the thoughts be as they may. And while I cannot say that you should do this in order to "get" something, you will indeed "get" something.

Oh, the joys of life's paradoxes!

Again, on one level, I fully grasp this, but at the same time, still struggle with it. Frankly, I am still addicted to being jacked on life. *How American, I know!* Yet, I am happy to put my faith in the deep tradition of Buddhism, and will continue cultivating this practice, attempting to stay balanced with the rhythms of life discussed earlier—*sleep* and *wakefulness*, *summer* and *winter*, *happiness* and *sorrow*, and yes, *life* and *death*.

What I am now interested in is moving on to a topic that we have kicked around during a couple of our most recent bonfires, namely what you have called a "holistic worldview." It seems to be a topic that, the more I have meditated on, rings true on the most intuitive of levels. So let's unpack this notion a bit.

"Live in peace; and the God of love and peace will be with you."
~ 2 CORINTHIANS 13:11

Be well,

Michael

Letter 19

God and the Universe are One: Forming a Holistic Worldview

Michael,

The first creation narrative from the book of Genesis is the perfect place to begin a discussion about the universe's oneness with the Creator, as well as the Creator's oneness with the creation. In this beautiful piece of poetry, the entirety of the cosmos is said to be nonviolently spoken into existence by the one true God—day, night, celestial bodies, water, trees, plants, animals, and yes, humankind.[1] In fact, humanity is said to be made in God's very image: "*Male* and *female* he created them" (Gen 1:27b—emphasis mine). So, in a way, we are set apart from the rest of the universe in that we have a special connection with the Creator. *We bear God's*

---

1. Counter to the Babylonian creation myth, *Enuma Elish*, the Hebrew version involves no violence. This is important to note because at the time, the Babylonian version was the culturally dominant story. Hence, the majority of Middle Easterners believed that the gods were violent, and that humanity arose only because the gods violently dismembered each other. The first narrative from Genesis, however, critiques this notion. It states how creation occurs from essentially "nothing," or, if you follow the Lurianic Kabbalah, that the light of creation pours into the *tzimtzum*, or "vacant space." Either way, God does not need to slaughter other gods in order to create, rather, he simply "speaks" and voila, creation.

image. We are the species tasked with "knowing" God, the ones who shall ask the *how* and *why* questions. Yet, at the same time, the *entirety* of the cosmos indeed bears God's "fingerprint." Yes, God is in fact inside us, he is knowable by searching within, but God is also to be found all throughout the universe, in the wind and the trees and streams and birds of the air, in everything. He is the grounding of *all* being in fact.

God's creation is also good. Actually, it is very good (*tov tov* in Hebrew), and intrinsically so. Life is always better than non-life, existence always better than nonexistence. Beingness is to be cherished, as all beings are of God's good creation. Nothing is not so. Nothing—not the things we don't like, not the people we hate, nothing.

That is why, when it comes to our worldview, things must remain holistic, as everything stems from the same Source. Indeed, nothing exists apart from God. And no matter what truth we discover about the cosmos, no matter what language we use to describe Reality, every truth will point in the same direction—*toward* a supremely benevolent God.

That said, when we turn to some of the doctrines floating around out there, doctrines we ourselves once held to, we should note that most fall short of this standard. Most pay no mind to any holism whatsoever. Take, for instance, the doctrine of ECT (or even, to a slightly lesser degree, CI). Whether the Calvinist or Arminian version, neither seems to strongly consider how any dualistic "ending" contradicts the oneness of the *tov tov* creation. That is to say, whereas the Hebrew poet talks about *all* of creation being *very good*, the doctrine of ECT states otherwise, as a place or state of objective horror can never be called "good." Not if language has any meaning.

Reconciliation to this conundrum happens, however, when we introduce Universalism. No longer do we have the cosmological dilemma of a split universe, where some are fortunate enough to forever enjoy God's good creation while others are trapped in objective terror over it, or done away with altogether. Instead, Reality retains its oneness, and not only that, but the cosmos "evolves" from *tov tov* ("very good") to *tov tov tov* ("perfected"). This is the picture the Apostle Paul paints in 1 Corinthians 15:24–26, 28 (all emphasis mine):

> Then comes the end, when he [Jesus Christ] hands over the kingdom to God the Father, after he has destroyed *every* ruler and *every* authority and power. For he must reign until he has put *all* his enemies under his feet. The last enemy to be destroyed is death . . . When *all* things are subjected to him, then the Son himself will also be subjected to the one who put *all* things in subjection under him, so that God may be *all* in *all*.

Quite fitting, then, is the Christian notion of a "collaborative eschatology," which states that the restored ending we are anxiously awaiting is actually brought about with our help (John Dominic Crossan). In other words, we pray for "thy kingdom come," and then we bring it about. Here's N.T. Wright on the matter:

> Because the early Christians believed that resurrection had begun with Jesus and would be completed in the great final resurrection on the last day, they believed also that God had called them to work with him, in the power of the spirit, to implement the achievement of Jesus and thereby anticipate the final resurrection, in personal and political life, in mission and holiness. If Jesus, the Messiah, was God's future arriving in person in the present, then those who belonged to Jesus and followed him in the power of his spirit were charged with transforming the present, as far as they were able, in the light of that future.[2]

Again, counter to this holistic view would be most of Western Christian eschatology—doctrines like the Rapture (John Nelson Darby), in which believers are sucked up through their exit hatches to go party with Jesus in the sky, while those "left behind" eventually end up boiling in a huge lake of fire. *Might I ask*: where is the holism here, or in any views similar to this? How does a Western view of heaven and hell fit with the first creation

---

2. Wright, *Surprised by Scripture*, 48–49.

narrative in Genesis? How does it fit with a cosmos that is "very good?" Or "very, very good" as we anticipate it becoming? How does this fit with the anthropological reality of humanity's individualism that we explored in our very first letter (René Girard)? Or the modern psychological truth, which states how we are so interconnected, that we start imitating "mommy" the moment we exit the womb (Andrew Meltzoff and M. Keith Moore)? Or the modern cosmological truth, which states that subatomic particles pass through our bodies and into other bodies, that they become entangled in such a way that neither time nor space seem to matter, and that everything in this great big universe is intertwined so much so that we could never begin to unravel it all (Max Planck, Niels Bohr, et al)? Are we even considering the oneness of creation at all when we hold to such anomalous doctrines?

It seems the answer, more often than not, is a resounding "no!"

Pity, really.

This all leads me to my final point, which is my most important. Our worldview, whether holistic or otherwise, very much matters to how we engage with our fellow human. It will inform our ethics, and greatly so. If we believe humans will be cast off to reside in some parallel universe called hell, or wiped out of existence altogether, it will, broadly speaking, fundamentally change how we view them. And if we believe we are *not* all one, that we are *not* all children of God, beloved and cherished eternally, then we will behave quite dissimilarly than if we did. Not for nothing, but those who inflict the most suffering on others seem to hold to a worldview that states we indeed are *not* one. The members of ISIS, for example, are not arguing for a worldview that says we are all a part of a cosmic consciousness, or that we will all one day be reconciled with each other and Allah. No! They state that the enemies of Allah will suffer eternally for their transgressions, cut off from God and from other humans, forever and ever. Deservedly so, too! And that is not to say all folks who have beliefs like this will end up being radicalized terrorists—of course not!—but it is to say radicalized terrorists seem to only spawn from a worldview such as the one they have. It would seem like a ridiculous notion for anyone proclaiming cosmic oneness to then go about killing others and inflicting all sorts of terror.

So do a thought experiment for me. Ask yourself how different things would be if everyone held to the view that all beings are eternally connected and secure, and that anything that suggests otherwise is mere delusion or illusion? Imagine if we all accepted the truth that the fundamental building block of Reality was consciousness (Amit Goswami), and that we were not disconnected, but instead that we were all subjectively experiencing this one consciousness? Imagine how the world would change. Imagine how ethics would change. Politics. Our view of ecology. And so on and so forth.

Just imagine. Meditate on this. I'll do the same.

So now, with that, here we are dear friend, arriving at the end of our fellowship. This will be my final correspondence. I've enjoyed this discussion as much as I've enjoyed anything in life, and I'm a bit sad that it is coming to an end. But perhaps we'll pick this conversation back up at a later time. So, in the meantime, I'll leave you with the words of Gandalf, "Go in peace! I will not say: do not weep; for not all tears are an evil."[3]

All my love,

Matthew

---

3. Tolkien, *Return of the King*, 1007.

Letter 20

The World is "Out There"

Matthew,

My friend, writing these letters has shown me two things. First, it has exposed how little I know about philosophy and religion, and second, when it is all said and done, how little I actually care. This may be a testament to how much of a Buddhist I really am. As Gandalf told Bilbo in *The Hobbit: An Unexpected Journey*, "The world is not in your books and maps, it's out there."[1] Indeed, nothing said about reality is ever reality itself. You'll only gather so much from hearing me talk about hiking Mt. Lassen, for example, but you'll actually know what I'm talking about if you join me in scaling it.

    I do not posses this apathy toward intellectual matters because I fail to find the topics interesting. And I dare not suggest books have no place in life. Quite the opposite! I am on the apathetic side because I have seen that I do not need philosophies and religion to fully know and appreciate what life is all about. After all, the thing itself is always more authoritative than that which points to it, and books are but the latter. Sadly, many people—folks who think like John Piper and Mark Driscoll, for instance—torture and reimagine common sense meanings of love, grace, justice, etc., clattering on

---

1. From *The Hobbit: An Unexpected Journey*.

and on in their beloved books, forcing their meanings to fly in the face of my direct experience. I know what such things as love and grace are because I have experienced them directly, so when I'm told that love and grace are contrary to this—as in, when love and grace are embedded in an economy of exchange, when they are reserved for some cherished "elect" only—I certainly must pause and sometimes even scoff. Why? Let me answer analogously: only a cartographer—a person who has either been to or seen a region—can draw an accurate map. And Bilbo can only write *There and Back Again: a Hobbit's Tale*, if he went there and back again. Likewise, only one who has lived in and experienced the world of unadulterated and unconditional grace can authoritatively talk about what it is like to live in that world.

If nothing else, I need a break from all the chatter, from all the mapmaking. This world that you and I have been a part of—let's call it intelligentsia at its best, pseudo-intelligentsia the rest of the time—is a loud and angry world. It is a world where people exert their selfhood through being correct, as Eckhart Tolle might put it.[2] It has grayed your hair and no doubt caused me to lose some of my own.

There are some things—*religion* and *effort*—I am done with for good. Some people say that effort and works are a natural outpouring of a grateful heart, and point to them as evidence that someone is saved. On the surface, I have no problem with that. I think it is easy to forget, though, that nothing has to be done in order to be saved, perhaps only undone. It would be odd, I admit, to find an individual who truly understood his position before the all-gracious God and yet did nothing to show their appreciation, but there is still grace for that. As the Apostle Paul said, "Where sin abounds, grace abounds all the more" (Rom 5:20). Indeed, it is the natural conclusion of a universe governed by grace. It is the reality of this situation that causes rejoicing, for nothing else is worthy, now that we've tasted it. And it is only within this situation that works find their proper place. So, if on any particular day I do not

---

2. See Tolle, Eckhart, *The Power of Now: a Guide to Spiritual Enlightenment*. Vancouver: Namaste, 1999.

feel like practicing meditation, or reading, or praying, then I won't. I have got all eternity to grow up.

Praise be to God for his grace!

To other things—friendship and good conversation—I hold fast. As long as there is wood to burn and topics to conquer there will be a seat for you at my *Bonfire Council*. I feel like I have found a priest in you, as well as a best friend. How many times throughout this project have I come to you with fear of my inadequacies as a writer? I am a bit embarrassed to say, but every time I have done this, I have been given nothing but encouragement. I'm far too lucky.

Goodbye for now. I have said what I feel I've earned the right to say, and I have nothing else to say at this present moment. I think I'll rest in meditation for a bit. Or, perhaps I'll go for a hike—but I repeat myself. I'll leave you with a prayer for peace, from Sufi mystic Pir-o-Murshid Inayat Khan.

> *Send thy peace O Lord,*
> *Which is perfect and everlasting, that our souls may radiate peace.*
> *Send thy peace O Lord,*
> *That we may think, act and speak harmoniously.*
> *Send thy peace, O Lord,*
> *That we may be contended and thankful for thy bountiful gifts.*
> *Send thy peace, O Lord,*
> *That we may endure all, tolerate all, in the thought of thy grace and mercy.*
> *Send thy peace O Lord,*
> *That our lives may become a divine vision and in thy light, all darkness may vanish.*
> *Send thy peace O Lord,*
> *Our Father and Mother, that we thy children on Earth may all unite in one family.*
> *Amen.*[3]

---

3. A collection of Khan's prayers can be found at http://www.towardtheone.com/prayers.htm.

Act IV: Exploring Reality

Namaste and shalom, and as always, as-salāmu ʿalaykum,

Michael

PS This Thursday, it's your turn to bring the wine. A nice red would do just fine.

Afterword

Moving Beyond Words

BY BEN FULLERTON

"Out beyond ideas of wrongdoing and rightdoing there is a field. I'll meet you there. When the soul lies down in that grass, the world is too full to talk about. Ideas, language, even the phrase 'each other' doesn't make sense."[1]

~ RUMI

Like many, I grew up in a fairly insulated cultural microcosm. Mine happened to be that of Western Evangelical Christianity, but this detail isn't the point. I was handed a box of things, and in it, assuredly, was the truth and nothing but the truth. Anything outside this box, no matter how well-intentioned, was not only false, but to be regarded as suspect if not downright dangerous.

I learned many things about what was in my box, and sometimes would question the contents therein, but really only to better understand them. Occasionally I would go so far as to listen to well

---

1. Rumi, *Essential Rumi*, 36.

educated folks who had a box just like mine give lectures on why this particular box was better than all the other boxes. And when I *did* encounter those who had been handed a different box, I never really sought to understand what was in it.

All along, the assumption was that I was carrying a box of truth. After all, this box was handed to me by those who knew and loved me. And it was handed to them in the same way. Surely, at one point, someone really dug deep and hard into this box and checked everything out—*right?*

Why even bother looking inside other boxes when I've already been handed the correct one?

As is often the case, my boxed-up worldview stayed fairly intact so long as I stayed in my cultural bubble. But as these things are wont to do, the wanderlust caught me and I eventually ventured out, both physically and philosophically.

Long had I been told by others what Jesus was all about, but at one I point really started to press him myself to try to better comprehend his ways. I began reading interpretations of him that were contrary to the ones I had been raised on, juggling the many different understandings in order to see which would stay in the air the longest.

Parallel to this, as a result of my obtuse posture and chronic back problems, I went seeking some comfort and stumbled my way into a yoga studio. Relief was found there, so I continued to go back and as I did, continued bumping into a smattering of Eastern teachings. "I'm just here for the back relief," I told myself, and did my best to tune it all out. Yet these words and fables from various wise teachers continued to bounce off my skull until some broke through, at which point they tumbled around and crashed into my neat little box.

One of the first to successfully besiege my strongholds was the fellow at the beginning of this essay—thirteenth-century Sufi mystic Rumi. As I continued to personally explore who Jesus was and what he was all about, and as I was hearing the words of a Sufi mystic while painfully stretching out my tired hamstrings, an uncomfortable and confusing reality started setting in—they were undeniably talking about the same thing. Now, this doesn't mean that all their teachings are identical or interchangeable, but when it comes to the nature of our existence, the ultimate reality behind this shrouded life, and the foundational Source of *love* that we call *God*, they were really just saying a different set of words and phrases that are meant to guide us to the same truth.

And this is when I realized something about my box. It wasn't a box of truth. Nay! It was a box of words. Phrases, lexicons, jargon, Christianese, conveniently simple closed loop answers to the infinitely nuanced house of mirrors we call reality; all of which when pressed to the breaking point of existential inquisition, become about as useful as trying to catch smoke with a butterfly net. Reality, however, couldn't fit inside my words. It couldn't fit inside my language and it certainly couldn't fit into my box.

You see, language is a really funny thing. It so efficiently makes us think that because we've maxed out our ability to put words behind something that we must now know what that thing is like. But we've become so entirely contented to sit in the hallway just outside the banquet, trading stories about what the feast must be like. Now and then, we bump into someone in the restroom who has actually spent time feasting in the banquet hall, and they tell us first-hand how marvelous the food is. "Indescribable!" they say. "Grander than anything you can imagine. You simply must go in and try it for yourself!"

So we leave the restroom and go back to the hallway, declaring "I've got it on good authority what the food is really like in there. Gather around and listen!" And we spin stories about its splendor, dreaming up even better words than we used before. We even go so far as to argue with the gentleman down the hall who describes the feast so differently. "What does he know anyway? I doubt he even ran into someone in the bathroom."

This is the product of living with a little theological box and is, by and large, how I've come to view all religious debates. We hang our hopes and dreams on the words of someone who heard from another what it's like at the banquet.

Moving Beyond Words

Yet, all throughout history, all around the world, teachers and guides have actually been to the banquet, glimpsed behind the curtain, seen into the heavenly places, and had the mind-altering *metánoia* of which Jesus spoke—the shift in perspective so radical that the entirety of existence, from the heavens to the earth and everything in between, looks completely different. And all of them, including our authors, come back saying the same thing: it's indescribable. The Love and Mercy and Compassion and Grace are all just too majestic to even describe! They still try their best to tell us, and we will hang on every word. But no description of a perfectly medium rare filet mignon will truly make sense to someone who has been sitting in the hallway listening to stories about food. One taste for yourself, however, and a vibrant reality that could never be contained in words becomes immediately clear. So put down your box and leave your words behind. Come and taste.

Namaste.

"I know that my spirit belongs to the Spirit of all Spirit. I know I belong to the city of those who have no place. But to find my way there, I need to let go of my knowing."[2]

~ RUMI

---

2. Rumi, *Little Book of Love*, 159.

Bibliography

Al-Arabi, Ibn. *Whoso Knoweth Himself.* Translated by W.H. Weir. Gloucestershire: Beshara, 1976.
Alison, James. *Knowing Jesus.* Springfield: Templegate, 1993.
Aquinas, Thomas. *The Summa Theologica of St. Thomas Aquinas.* Translated by the Fathers of the English Dominican Provinc. New York: Benzinger Bros., 1948.
Baker, Sharon L. *Executing God: Rethinking Everything You've Been Taught about Salvation and the Cross.* Louisville: Westminster John Knox, 2015.
Bartlett, Anthony. "Isaiah 53." In *The Jesus Driven Life: Reconnecting Humanity with Jesus.* Lancaster: JDL, 2010.
Becker, Ernest. *The Denial of Death.* New York: Free Press, 1973.
Bettenson, Henry, ed. *The Early Christian Fathers: A selection from the writings of the Fathers from St. Clement of Rome to St. Athanasius.* Oxford: Oxford University Press, 1956.
Bonhoeffer, Dietrich. *The Collected Sermons of Dietrich Bonhoeffer.* Edited by Isabel Best. Minneapolis: Fortress, 2012.
Bucke, Richard Maurice. *Cosmic Consciousness: A Study in the Evolution of the Human Mind.* Philadelphia: Innes, 1905.
Calvin, John. *Institutes of the Christian Religion.* Translated by Ford, Lewis, and Battles. Grand Rapids: Eerdmans, 1975.
Chesterton, G.K. *Orthodoxy.* Garden City: Doubleday, 1959.
Coulter, Ann. *If Democrats Had Any Brains, They'd Be Republicans.* New York: Three Rivers, 2007.
Distefano, Matthew J. *All Set Free: How God is Revealed in Jesus and Why that is Really Good News.* Eugene: Resource, 2015.
———. *From the Blood of Abel: Humanity's Root Causes of Violence and the Bible's Theological-Anthropological Solution.* Orange: Quoir, 2016.

Bibliography

———. "Love is." *The Raven ReView* (November 2015). https://www.ravenfoundation.org/love-is/.

Easwaran, Eknath, ed. *The Bhagavad Gita*. Tomales: Nilgiri, 1985.

Edwards, Jonathan. *The Works of President Edwards*. New York: Burt Franklin, 1968.

Girard, René. *I See Satan Fall Like Lightning*. Translated by James G. Williams. New York: Orbis, 2001.

———. *Things Hidden Since the Foundation of the World*. Translated by Stephen Bann and Michael Metteer. Stanford: Stanford University Press, 1978.

Halberstam, David. *The Making of a Quagmire*. New York: Random House, 1965.

Hardin, Michael. *The Jesus Driven Life: Reconnecting Humanity with Jesus*. 2nd Edition. Lancaster: JDL, 2013.

———. *Walking with Grandfather: A Skeptic's Journey to Spirituality*. Lancaster: JDL, 2014.

Hart, David Bentley. "Christ's Rabble: The First Christians Were Not Like Us." *Commonweal Magazine* (September 2016). https://www.commonwealmagazine.org/exchange-christs-rabble.

Hodgkinson, Tom. "Live Lazy, Live Long: Look at Britain's Oldest Man" *The Guardian* (November 2012). https://www.theguardian.com/commentisfree/2012/nov/05/live-long-lazy-britain-oldest-man.

Hughes, Glenn. "The Denial of Death and the Practice of Dying." *Ernest Becker Foundation* (2015). http://ernestbecker.org/?page_id=989.

Jersak, Brad. "Salted with Fire." *Christianity Without the Religion* (February 2016). http://christianity-without-the-religion.blogspot.com/2016/02/q-self-amputation-hellfire-mark-9-brad.html.

Kierkegaard, Søren. *Journals and Papers: Volume 6, Autobiographical, Part Two, 1848–1855*. Edited and Translated by Howard V. Hong and Edna H. Hong. Bloomington: Indiana University Press, 1978.

Lewis, C.S. *Out of the Silent Planet*. London: Pan, 1952.

———. *The Problem of Pain*. Revised ed. Edition. San Francisco: HarperOne, 2015.

MacDonald, George. *Unspoken Sermons*. Salt Lake City: Project Gutenberg, 2005.

Machuga, Michael. "Foreword." In *All Set Free: How God is Revealed in Jesus and Why That is Really Good News*. Eugene: Resource, 2015.

Machuga, Ric. *Three Theological Mistakes: How to Correct Enlightenment Assumptions about God, Miracles, and Free Will*. Eugene: Cascade, 2015.

Moltmann, Jürgen. *The Coming of God: Christian Eschatology*. Translated by Margaret Kohl. Minneapolis: Fortress, 2004.

———. *Theology of Hope: On the Ground and the Implications of a Christian Eschatology*. Translated by James W. Leitch. Minneapolis: Fortress, 1993.

Nasr, Seyyed Hossein. *Sufi Essays*. Albany: State University of New York Press, 1972.

Bibliography

Oughourlian, Jean-Michel. *The Genesis of Desire*. Translated by Eugene Webb. East Lansing: Michigan State University Press, 2010.

Pascal, Blaise. *Pensées*. Translated by W.F. Trotter. Seattle: Pacific, 2011.

Pearce, Jonathan. "Psychology of Religion: Religion—A Hell of a Lot of Fear and Depression." *A Tippling Philosopher* (April 2014). http://www.skepticink.com/tippling/2014/04/23/psychology-of-religion-religion-a-hell-of-a-lot-of-fear-and-depression/.

Plantinga Jr., Cornelius. *Not the Way It's Supposed to Be: A Breviary of Sin*. Grand Rapids: Eerdmans, 1995.

Polanyi, Michael. *The Tacit Dimension*. Chicago: University of Chicago Press, 1966.

Reitan, Eric. "Human Freedom and the Impossibility of Eternal Damnation." In *Universal Salvation? The Current Debate*. Edited by Robin Parry and Christopher Partridge. Grand Rapids: Eerdmans, 2004.

Rohr, Richard. *Everything Belongs: The Gift of Contemplative Prayer*. New York: Crossroad, 2003.

Rumi, Jalāl ad-Dīn Muhammad. *The Essential Rumi*. Translated by Coleman Barks. San Francisco: HarperSanFrancisco, 1995.

———. *Rumi's Little Book of Love: 150 Poems That Speak to the Heart*. Translated by Maryam Mafi and Azima Melita Kolin. San Antonio: Hierophant, 2014.

Singh, Sadhu Sundar. *Meditations on Various Aspects of the Spiritual Life*. London: Macmillan, 1926.

Talbott, Thomas. *The Inescapable Love of God*. 2nd Edition. Eugene: Cascade, 2014.

———. "Toward a Better Understanding of Universalism." In *Universal Salvation?: The Current Debate*, edited by Robin Parry and Christopher Partridge. Grand Rapids: Eerdmans, 2003.

The Hobbit: An Unexpected Journey, DVD. Directed by Peter Jackson. Produced by Cunningham, Weiner, et al. Burbank: Warner, 2012.

Tolkien, J.R.R. *The Fellowship of the Ring*. New York: Ballantine, 1982.

———. *The Return of the King: Being the Third Part of The Lord of the Rings*. New York: Houghton Mifflin, 1955.

Tolle, Eckhart. *The Power of Now: A Guide to Spiritual Enlightenment*. Vancouver: Namaste, 1999.

Watts, Alan. *The Book: On the Taboo Against Knowing Who You Are*. New York: Vintage, 1966.

———. *The Culture of Counter culture: The Edited Transcripts*. North Clarendon: Tuttle, 1999.

———. *The Essence of Alan Watts*. Berkeley: Celestial Arts, 1977.

———. *Still the Mind: An Introduction to Meditation*. Novato: New World, 2002.

———. *The Tao of Philosophy*. North Clarendon: Tuttle, 1999.

———. *The Way of Zen*. New York: Vintage, 1999.

———. *The Wisdom of Insecurity: A Message for an Age of Anxiety*. New York: Vintage, 1951.

BIBLIOGRAPHY

Weil, Simone. *First and Last Notebooks: Supernatural Knowledge*. Translated by Richard Rees. Eugene: Wipf & Stock, 2015.

Williams, Donald T. *Mere Humanity: G.K. Chesterton, C.S. Lewis, and J.R.R. Tolkien on the Human Condition*. Nashville: Broadman & Holman, 2006.

Zahnd, Brian. "God is Like Jesus." *BrianZahnd.com* (August 2011). http://brianzahnd.com/2011/08/god-is-like-jesus-2/.

www.ingramcontent.com/pod-product-compliance
Lightning Source LLC
Chambersburg PA
CBHW071436160426
43195CB00013B/1928

"Correspondence between friends is always illuminating. Here, Distefano and Machuga tackle issues close to the heart: what it means to be human, why religion does not work, and why a careful ear for listening to each other is essential to both friendship and knowledge. This is a truly fascinating read of two younger adults navigating their way into post-modernity."

—**Michael Hardin**, Executive Director, Preaching Peace, author of *The Jesus Driven Life*

"This book is about the collapse of a Christian worldview, the one that says the thing Jesus saves from is an eternal hell of torment. The anxieties and contradictions of this kind of theology are too awful to sustain, and *A Journey With Two Mystics* lays them all out with autobiographical clarity in a gentle epistolary exchange between two friends, Distefano and Machuga. Gentle but charged with consequence, one which might aptly be named *Either Nike or Krisis!*, Machuga finds relief from violent religion in a form of Buddhism where the point of life is the joyous peaceful now: there is no ulterior goal to human activity (e.g. heaven), so he quotes approvingly the brand's iconic tagline, "Just do it!" Distefano sees Jesus as opening up the divine space of a new nonviolent humanity. The New Testament word *krisis* is translated judgment with all the fearful connotations of an eternal destiny in heaven or hell. But Distefano sees it as God's compassionate transformation of existence which, nevertheless, can still be reversed by the actual horrors of catastrophic human violence. Is there a real difference between the two friends? Even they seem unsure, but the reader is invited to discover an answer for herself in this extraordinarily rich and resonant conversation."

—**Anthony W. Bartlett**, author of *Virtually Christian* and *Pascale's Wager*

"Reading this book is like getting an accessible crash course in a range of interconnected ideas about the human predicament and the promise of salvation. But not the kind of course you'd get in a classroom. It's more like the voyeuristic pleasure of listening in on two friends, animated by philosophical and theological ideas, passionately sharing their thoughts by a bonfire. In fact, that's exactly how this book was born."

—**Eric Reitan**, Oklahoma State University

"We are living through a post-Christian moment. The older, violent versions of American fundamentalism and evangelicalism are no longer compelling for many who grew up under their tutelage. The mainline churches long ago lost most of their young adults and are struggling to find their footing in the Good News. A new group of faith explorers from both traditions is emerging. They are not necessarily giving up on their Christian faith, but reframing it and renewing it. In this book you are invited to listen in on a thrilling conversation between two of these pilgrims, one a follower of René Girard and the other a fan of Alan Watts. Perhaps you will overhear your own story. Perhaps you too will find your faith renewed."

—**John E. Phelan, Jr.**, Senior Professor of Theological Studies, North Park Theological Seminary

"From Buddhism to Christianity to René Girard to Alan Watts to Gandalf—this book is full of profound wisdom. Distefano and Machuga are excellent guides to the truth found in these traditions. As Distefano states, 'No matter what truth we discover about the cosmos . . . every truth will point in the same direction—toward a supremely benevolent God.' So, sit in your favorite chair, grab a cup of coffee or a glass of wine, and join these mystics as they dive into the love of the divine."

—**Adam Ericksen**, Education Director, The Raven ReView; blogger, Teaching Nonviolent Atonement on Patheos

"True to the mystic tradition, Distefano and Machuga set out to authentically explore the dynamic, transformational inner journey of faith. Using a personal, engaging style of correspondence, together they tackle many of the distorted-over-time conservative Christian teachings and doctrines that have finally and thankfully began to unravel, offering more reasonable and palatable interpretations of the universally human spiritual path."

—**Julie Ferwerda**, author of *Raising Hell*

"*A Journey With Two Mystics* was just as I expected it to be: an intellectually honest and humble interchange between two close friends. Although they do not see eye-to-eye on every theological and philosophical point, they respect and cherish the opinion of the other.

They have obviously been freed to test all things so that they may hold onto what is both good and true. This book is the result of a peace that truly surpasses all understanding."

—**Charles Watson Sr.**, author of *Hell in a Nutshell*

"Distefano and Machuga—two friends sharing a common quest for peace in our world—invite us to an intriguing exchange of letters. René Girard meets Alan Watts—West meets East. Here the insecure human ego and individualism of our culture opens to self in other as their conversation joins the God of grace and salvation in Jesus Christ to the cosmic oneness of reconciliation and peace."

—**David R. Froemming**, ELCA pastor; author of *Salvation Story*

"In this new age of Christian enlightenment, Distefano and Machuga offer a powerful and fresh conversation that goes to the core of life's true meaning. In addition to being uniquely written and refreshingly real, the dialogue offers savory insights that are critical to integrate into the Jesus tradition of our day, such as mindfulness, Universalism, and the naked now. These two mystics will have you continually wanting to flip to the next page."

—**Eric Alexander**, founder of *Jesism*

"Theology is like sex: it's deeply personal, soul revealing, and no one wants to be told they are doing it wrong. In *A Journey With Two Mystics*, we are given a rare window into the depths of mind and heart of two great theologians who courageously and eloquently wrestle with the most important questions concerning God, ourselves, and life. The vulnerability, fearless exploration, and mutual respect offered in this literary work of theological art is a monumental gift to those who think, dialogue, and pursue a greater understanding about all things God."

—**Chris Kratzer**, pastor, blogger

"Reading through *A Journey With Two Mystics* is a delightful and entertaining opportunity to eavesdrop (by invitation, of course) on a conversation between two lifelong friends, in which they discuss some of the things that matter most: theology, humanity, culture, literature, and even heaven and hell. You may not always agree with Distefano and Machuga. In fact, they don't always agree with each other. But that's not the point. The point is sitting around the bonfire with your best friend on a Thursday night, learning to follow Jesus together, one step at a time, on a journey that never ends."

—**Daniel Skillman**, counselor, writer, teacher, speaker